Ways of Grace

Ways *of* Grace

Stories of Activism, Adversity,
and How Sports Can Bring Us Together

James Blake

with Carol Taylor

Amistad
An Imprint of HarperCollins*Publishers*

A hardcover edition of this book was published in 2017
by Amistad, an imprint of HarperCollins Publishers.

HarperCollins books may be purchased for educational, business,
or sales promotional use. For information, please email the Special
Markets Department at SPsales@harpercollins.com.

FIRST AMISTAD PAPERBACK EDITION PUBLISHED 2018.

Designed by Suet Yee Chong

Library of Congress Cataloging-in-Publication Data has been
applied for.

ISBN 978-0-06-235453-2 (pbk.)

18 19 20 21 22   LSC   10 9 8 7 6 5 4 3 2 1

To anyone who has ever chosen to take a stand
for something greater than themselves

Contents

Ways of Grace

INTRODUCTION

Mistaken Identity

I t is a funny thing the moment when your perception of the world changes. It's not that anything in reality has actually changed, it is your perception of the world and how you are perceived in it that has been forever indelibly and irrevocably altered. That life-changing moment happened to me September 9, 2015, on a sunny Wednesday afternoon as I stood outside my hotel near a bustling Grand Central Terminal. I was in New York and on my way to the US Open tournament to do corporate appearances for my role as chairman of the United States Tennis Association (USTA) Foundation.

I have played tennis for most of my thirty-six years, professionally since 1999. My parents loved the game and they passed that love on to me and my older brother, Thomas. My mother, Betty, is British, and my father, Tom, was African American. They met on the court and fell in love playing the game. My mother is in her eighties and she still plays once or twice a week. My oldest daughter is a toddler and already has a racket. I started playing tennis with Thomas and my parents when I was five years old. I began taking lessons when I was ten or eleven. When I turned thirteen I decided to quit other sports and focus exclusively on tennis. That was a suggestion from my dad—not for tennis specifically, but just to pick one thing and be good at it. At that time I was all over the place, as any energetic teenager would be. I had hobbies and loved sports of all kind. Dad told me, "You're doing a bunch of things; why don't you pick one and try to really excel at it?" I decided on tennis because I felt I was the best at it, but I also liked the individual aspect of it. Being a professional tennis player is like being an entrepreneur. All the decisions fall to me, but I can customize my game, my training, and my approach, which suits my personality.

Every weekend my parents, Thomas, and I would leave our house in Yonkers and head to Harlem to play. Even when we moved from Yonkers up to Connecticut, on the weekends we still headed down to the courts in Harlem. When I turned seventeen, I followed my brother to Harvard. I played on the tennis team for two years, from 1997 to 1999. After being approached by an agent my sophomore year, I decided to go pro and play professionally.

Over the course of my career as a pro tennis player I was among the top four players in the world, and a Davis Cup champion. During that time I wrote my memoir, *Breaking Back*, about the challenges I faced coming back from a traumatic injury and overcoming a family tragedy. Those fourteen years taught me how to persevere not only on the court but also off the court, as I overcame many challenging professional and personal issues. I retired from pro tennis in 2013. In 2015 I became chairman of the USTA Foundation, which is the charitable arm of the association. My role as chairman keeps me connected to the game I love so much and allows me to stay involved in a very positive way.

As I stood waiting for the car to arrive to take me to the US Open for sponsor appearances and USTA Foundation meetings I saw a man running toward me. He reminded me of one of my friends from high school. Freshman year I was on the wrestling team with several seniors. I was the tiniest one. The seniors would pick me up and throw me around. It was fun, and what you'd expect from teenaged boys. They were wrestlers, so they would wrestle me, and joke around.

A few days earlier my friend had written on my website, "Hey! I haven't seen you in twenty years, just checking in. We're all proud of you." I was glad to hear from him. Considering that he had been a senior when I was a freshman, he was pretty nice to me in high school. He was a big guy too, with a shaved head. As I stood there, in front of the Grand Hyatt, in Midtown Manhattan, three days after hearing from him, I saw a guy running toward me. He had a bald head, and was a big guy. What a coincidence to see him there, I thought, and I smiled. When he reached me he picked me up and slammed me to the ground. The next thing I know, he's sitting on top of me, yanking my arms behind my back and handcuffing me.

At this point I knew it was not my friend from school and I figured out that despite his not wearing a badge or identifying himself as a cop, he must be one, because he had handcuffs. Despite what you may have heard about New York, I couldn't imagine I was being robbed in broad daylight outside Grand Central. As I lay on the ground, my face pressed into the concrete, going through my head was, *Oh my god, this is wrong!*

That's when I tried to remember everything I had heard from the news about resisting arrest, though I had no idea what I was being arrested for. From all the media and news reports of tragic police incidents, I knew there were far worse things that could happen to me during a confrontation with law enforcement. I said, "I'm cooperating, whatever you say. I'm complying a hundred percent, whatever you say." That's when he yanked me up and walked me over to five men several feet away. Though they weren't in uniform, I assumed they were officers because they had badges visible on their belts.

"This is a mistake. This is an absolute mistake, you guys have the wrong person," I said as I stood handcuffed in the middle of the sidewalk.

"Okay," one officer said, though he made no move to release me, and they still hadn't told me why I was handcuffed or what they were looking for. Another officer asked for ID. I indicated that he should look in my pocket. The officer took out my driver's license, and said, "We have witnesses that tell us that you were involved in criminal activity."

"Witnesses? What are you talking about?"

"Someone said he's been delivering things to you for the last two weeks."

None of this was making any sense. "I'm staying in this hotel," I told him. "We can go up to my room. I'll show you the plane ticket. I arrived on a red-eye flight this morning. There is no way that I could have been doing anything here for two weeks, when I just got in this morning."

The plainclothes officer who had tackled me and was still holding me by the arm was not very open to what I was saying. He just repeated, "We'll see. We'll see. We'll figure this out. We'll see."

I kept telling them, "Look, this has nothing to do with me." I pleaded with them to look at my US Open badge in my back pocket. At this point it was hanging out. "Please, look at my badge, you can tell that I'm not a criminal. I have a badge for the US Open. I was on my way there now."

"Okay, we'll see. We'll see."

They still wouldn't take the badge out. They didn't believe me until about ten minutes later when another officer, an older man, arrived on the scene. As I watched him examine my ID I could see that he realized there was a problem. After he looked at my license and I told him that I was a professional tennis player and was heading to the Open, he took out his phone and appeared to be looking something up. Then he looked again at my ID and what must have been a picture of me on his phone. That's when he apologized and had the other officers uncuff me. He was the only one, of the five or six officers there, who apologized. The officer who tackled me, whose last name I later found out is Frascatore, never did.

At that moment my car arrived and I walked away in a daze and got in. I didn't ask for any badge numbers or their names. I didn't ask for their precinct information. I was just relieved to be away from them. The full effect of what occurred in those fifteen minutes hadn't yet sunk in. I was still in shock. I had not fully processed what just happened to me on a busy New York City sidewalk. I still didn't fully realize that I'd been manhandled and handcuffed, then dragged to my feet in full view of crowds of people streaming by. And I was completely innocent. I was just relieved to be away from them and that scene and ready to forget it. I sat in the car still shaken, then called my wife, Emily, and told her what happened.

"I just want to forget about it," I said. "I almost can't even believe it."

"What if that had happened to me?" she asked, her voice trembling with anger.

When I thought about it, I couldn't even imagine it.

"You have to do something. You can't just let it go."

As she spoke, her hurt and indignation for me seeped into my stunned brain. That's when I got angry. I started to shake just thinking of my wife, a member of my family, or anyone I loved being treated the way I had just been treated. The shock was subsiding, and as my mind cleared I knew that what had taken place was wrong and I had to do something about it. But what was I going to do?

I decided to give an interview about what happened with the press at the Open.

That afternoon, the police department issued a statement, which wasn't surprising since my interview had just hit the airwaves online in the media. What *was* surprising was the statement they issued. Although the officers on the scene admitted that something had occurred, their version of the events was very different from mine. They claimed that I was detained for less than a minute, was not manhandled, and that I was never in handcuffs. I couldn't believe it, but it was the word of five officers against mine.

I went down to the hotel lobby to find the head of security. I asked if there were surveillance cameras outside the hotel.

He said there were. I explained what happened and we went to his office and watched the video. As I watched it play out I said to him, "The officers are claiming that I was detained for a minute and that I wasn't tackled or handcuffed."

He pointed to the time at the bottom of the screen. "We have the time stamp on it. You were detained for twelve minutes. You were in cuffs for ten minutes."

I watched the video a second time. It was as if I needed to see it again to believe that what I *knew* happened had actually happened. I saw myself leaning on the building. I saw Officer Frascatore tackle me and throw me to the ground. I saw him kneeling on my back as he yanked my arms behind me and cuffed me. I saw him pull me to my feet and walk me out of view. Then I thought about their statement that none of it happened.

I decided to go to the press, and I did an interview with *Good Morning America* the next day. It was important to me to tell my side of the story as it actually happened. Three days later the NYPD called a press conference, and William Bratton, the police commissioner, released a statement. This time the officers' version of the events had changed. Their statement was now a lot closer to what had actually occurred. The police had obtained the surveillance video from the hotel not long after I viewed it, but they did not immediately release it. I found out in the statement that Officer Frascatore was put on desk duty pending an investigation.

It should not matter that I am a tennis star, or a public figure with access to the media, to be treated respectfully and not have my rights taken for granted by law enforcement. All people, regardless of race, gender, religion, sexual orientation, or perceived socioeconomic standing, should know that police officers will treat them respectfully and issue an accurate and timely report of any incident or altercation between them and law enforcement.

That I have a platform and access to the media should not make what happened to me any more significant. No one should be manhandled without due process and definitely not because of a vague likeness to someone else. Even if I were the man they were looking for, why would such excessive force be necessary if I was cooperating? This speaks to a larger issue in America, the use of excessive force by law enforcement, especially against minorities. From what we see in the media and read in the paper, it is clear that there are a few police officers in our country who think that having a badge makes them above the law.

My grandfather, whom I was named after, was a New York police officer, and I am extremely proud of him for his service. But not all officers are like him. Officers who don't have regard for the public they serve make it worse for the overwhelming majority of police officers who are working hard to do their jobs respectfully and sensitively, even as they put their lives on the line to protect and to serve. Those men and women are truly heroes. I know, because that's the type of police officer my grandfather was. These officers make the streets safer; they protect us from harm, at times putting their own lives in jeopardy for ours. This is why I hold the police force in high regard.

My wife's words led me to realize something had to be done about it, that it wasn't right. If I were heading off to work and it happened to me, after being released I would have had to rush to get to my job because now I would have been late. It would be a lot less likely that I would be able to figure out later who the officers on the scene were, or why they detained me. And without any video evidence, I would have no recourse. More than likely, I would just be happy to be able to walk away, even if I had to live with the humiliation of the encounter.

When I did speak out, it was my word against theirs. The word of five police officers who all said nothing had happened. That's what I faced before they knew about the surveillance video. Regardless of what the officers said, the video took priority, because you could see the events as they unfolded. You could *see* it.

When releasing the video, the police commissioner spoke on the record and said it was a case of mistaken identity and that the suspect could have been my twin. However, the photo of the person they showed during the press conference was an Australian national who was not in the US at the time. Misinformation and a lack of reporting by the offending officers and their superiors is a second violation against victims. When you consider that the average citizen does not have the resources or the platform to fight this type of manipulation and cover-up, it is not surprising that more of these instances of excessive force or misconduct do not see the light of day.

Before the video was released, I told some close friends about what happened. These were people who knew me, who knew that I am not one to exaggerate. Of course they were upset about it. Their responses ranged from "Aw, that's terrible," to "Oh, that stinks." Once they saw the video, though, they called me back in shock. They had not realized the severity of the encounter. They did not really believe that the officer had charged me and slammed me to the ground, handcuffed and detained me, and that I was literally standing there doing nothing when it happened. Even people who know me well thought I must have been doing something to have been handled so forcefully. I have a buddy who even joked about it until he saw the video. After watching it he said that it actually made him sick to see something like that happen to a friend. Before seeing the video account, my friends didn't believe the severity of the incident. Honestly, why would they? It seems almost unbelievable.

I thought about all the incidents in the media of police misconduct, racial profiling, and discriminatory practices, and I wondered how many of them actually happened the way the officers reported it. How many times had officers not reported an incident at all? I wondered how many times innocent men and women managed to walk away and how many times they had not. When I think back to that day I can't help but consider how badly it could have turned out if only a few things had gone differently.

I was tackled, handcuffed, paraded down a crowded sidewalk, and detained for twelve minutes before the officers realized they had the wrong man. Officer Frascatore did not identify himself as a member of law enforcement, ask my name, read me my rights, or in any way afford me the dignity and respect due every person who walks the streets of this country. While I believe the vast majority of our police officers are dedicated public servants who conduct themselves appropriately, I know that what happened to me is sadly not uncommon. This became even more significant when I read in a 2015 *New York Times* article about the incident titled "Officer Who

Arrested James Blake Has History of Force Complaints" that Frascatore had at least three other complaints of using excessive force.[1] You have to wonder if those three reports are really forty, or a hundred, because he did not report them in the same way he had not reported mine.

Too often in the recent past, we have watched videos of sometimes fatal encounters with the police that have sparked international outrage. One can only wonder how these victims would have been portrayed in the media without video evidence. One also wonders how many other victims exist that we will never hear about. I am sure many were not as innocent as I may have been, but I cannot imagine any of them, or really anyone, being deserving of such a level of excessive force. According to the *Times* article, Frascatore's other alleged victims, who filed complaints of excessive force, claimed to have been punched either in the mouth, the stomach, or the temple. One claimed to have been thrown to the ground and pummeled. Many average citizens do not have a platform with the media, or an opportunity to uncover incidents like mine, which makes me know it is vital for me to speak up.

Two years later the incident is still with me, and I am forever changed by it. I've spent some of those years wondering how to address it, the injustice of it, as it relates not only to me but to anyone who has had a run-in or altercation with law enforcement. Think of all the people who were minding their own business and then found themselves unfairly and unjustly detained, harassed, mistreated, embarrassed, victimized, or worse. I can't imagine how many times something like a case of mistaken identity, of being in the wrong place at the wrong time, or worse, a case of racial profiling or discrimination, could and has happened. I wonder how often indignities like that occur, to innocent people who do not have the means or a platform to tell their side of the story.

I also wanted to use my voice and my role as an athlete to make a difference, to turn this unfortunate incident into a catalyst for change in the relationship between the police and the public they serve, in a way that would be helpful to both. But for many months I wondered if I was the right person to do it. I'm an athlete, not an activist. Why would anyone care about what I have to say off the tennis court? Then I thought about a man who has been an inspiration to me. Arthur Ashe inspired me as a tennis player. He was also one of the greatest activists of his generation. A man of many firsts on and off the court, Ashe was the first African American to win the men's singles at Wimbledon and the US Open, and the first black American to be ranked number one in the world. Using his platform, Ashe pushed to create inner-city tennis programs for teens, and he was an advocate against apartheid in South Africa. He even obtained a visa so he could visit and play tennis there to inspire the people of the country.

As exemplary a tennis player as he was, Ashe was also inspirational for how he conducted himself outside tennis. For the last fourteen years of his life Ashe had major health issues. In 1979 he underwent a quadruple bypass operation and then a second bypass in 1983. In 1988, after experiencing paralysis in his right arm, he had brain surgery. A biopsy revealed that Ashe had AIDS. He'd contracted HIV from a transfusion of bad blood during his second heart operation in 1983.

Even during those dark times, Arthur Ashe never asked "Why me?" Ashe believed that to ask "Why me?" of the bad things in your life is to ask "Why me?" of the good things in your life. To him, it was unrealistic to not expect the bad with the good. "I wasn't saying why me when I'm holding up the Wimbledon trophy. You can't say why me when something bad happens when you have so many good things," Ashe often said. That is one of the reasons why he is such a role model to me. Instead of focusing on his medical issues, he decided to bring attention to HIV/AIDS, which at that time was widely misunderstood. Although weakened by the illness, Ashe worked tirelessly to raise awareness and battle misperceptions about AIDS and HIV. In 1992, despite his deteriorating health, he went to Washington, DC, to march in protest over the United States' treatment of Haitian refugees. During the protest he was arrested and taken away in handcuffs. That image of him being led away is forever burned in my mind.

"Start where you are. Use what you have. Do what you can." Arthur Ashe embodied those words. He imbued everything he did with passion, pathos, humility, and humanity. He left a lasting impact not only on the game of tennis but also on our country, and on the entire world. His words, and really his life, served as the impetus for me to try to make a difference. It did not matter who I was, or what I did. All that mattered was that I used what I had and did what I could.

Ways of Grace was inspired by Ashe's memoir, *Days of Grace*. Illuminating and insightful, his life story is a testament to how moments of adversity can actually move you in a direction of grace, and how you can respond to life in a graceful way as opposed to a reactionary, divisive way. Ashe showed us that we can use adversity to heal and not to hurt; we can use it to unite and not to divide. When Ashe was a Wimbledon champion he was fighting apartheid. He was fighting for those who were less fortunate. He was fighting for people who were in a bad situation that he had the ability and the resources to help.

When Ashe was facing insurmountable physical odds, when he had HIV, when he contracted AIDS, he was helping others who did not have the same treatment that he had, who did not have the money he had, who did not have the voice or the platform that he had. Even as he struggled, he sought to help the cause of HIV/AIDS research. Ashe taught me that despite the situation you are in, no matter how grave, how embarrassing, or how devastating, you can try to find a positive way to affect the world. As I considered Ashe and his profound impact on not only sports but also the world, I considered other sports figures who have sparked change, on the field and off. I wanted to bring to light their stories of activism, advocacy, and courage even as they faced a harsh personal, societal, and financial backlash. As I researched, I was struck by how many athletes—past and present—have championed causes they are passionate about and have created change in positive and uplifting ways, publicly and privately. I want to tell their stories.

Sports have always united us—regardless of race, religion, gender, or sexual orientation—as we come together to cheer for and support our hometown, state, or country. When we root for our favorite team, athlete, or sport, it is not race, gender, or religious affiliation that unites us. It is our appreciation of an athlete's ability to perform—sometimes against overwhelming odds—to rise up from poverty, from war, from divisiveness, from even disability, to advance to the top of his or her sport and to excel, sometimes beyond one's wildest hopes or dreams.

The journey of athletes not only to overcome their competitors but often to overcome themselves—their backgrounds, their own physical or emotional shortcomings—to be the best they can be, has inspired us since the first Olympic Games in 776 BC. Sports brings different people, different countries, different nationalities, different races, and different religions together, even the most divided. The Olympics became an international event in 1924, unifying countries, even if only for a short time, as athletes from all around the world compete with each other in a mutually tolerant and respectful way. For decades it was the only time historically warring and divisive nations and countries came together peacefully.

Athletes have inspired us throughout history. They have changed not only their respective games, but also the world around them. Some of them have done so in a big way, in front of a crowd of millions, like Billie Jean King. Formerly ranked the number one tennis player, King is also a longtime activist for sexual and gender equality and for equal prize money in tournaments. King not only championed the cause that women could compete on the same level as men, she also proved it. In the Astrodome in Houston, Texas, in the game-changing 1973 "Battle of the Sexes" match, King beat the former number one men's champion (and self-proclaimed male chauvinist) Bobby Riggs, and the crowd rose to their feet in support of her achievement. Her success that day and over the course of her tremendous career paved the way for equality for all female athletes.

Many of us are familiar with the epic stand that Tommie Smith and John Carlos took during the 1968 Mexico City Summer Olympics. Standing on the podium in the gold and bronze positions, they bowed their heads and raised their fists while "The Star-Spangled Banner" played. They were showing support for human rights and equality and taking a stand for civil liberties. Although they are now celebrated for their contributions to civil rights, the repercussions of their protest haunted them for decades. There was a third man on the podium whose selfless support and contribution to their protest has all but disappeared from history. A white Australian, Peter Norman, the silver winner, is rarely credited for his support in that riveting moment, but he played a crucial role and faced harsh criticism and severe backlash because of it.

Although not as well known, Norman's role in advancing equality and human rights was just as monumental and inspiring as that of his colleagues on the podium next to him. Back in Australia, the ramifications of his protest were just as devastating—if not more—as what Carlos and Smith faced, but Norman never recovered from it, and the story of the part he played is not often told.

For weeks it was impossible to turn on the television or go on social media without seeing an image of the former San Francisco 49ers quarterback Colin Kaepernick kneeling during the national anthem to protest police brutality, while everyone stood around him. His protest has rippled far beyond the football stadium as it gained momentum, in sometimes surprising ways. However, not many people are aware of the former Denver Nuggets guard Mahmoud Abdul-Rauf praying during the national anthem in 1996, twenty years earlier. He is a precursor to athletes like Kaepernick, who made the same decision to take a stand against what he felt was unjust. The moment Kaepernick went down on one knee on the football field he made a choice that has since become historic.

We may know of the sports figures like King, Smith, Carlos, and now Kaepernick whose contributions shook the world and changed not only their sport but also how athletes are perceived. There are so many other sports figures who are inciting change in smaller, quieter, yet no less tangible and far-reaching ways. I hope to shed light on the part Norman, Abdul-Rauf, and other, lesser-known activists, accidental and not, played in making history, in their own quiet yet no less inspiring and courageous ways.

While professional athletes can make a significant amount of money in a fairly short time, a slump, an injury, a trade, or getting cut from the team can change things in an instant. These are considerations every professional athlete who decides to speak out for a cause must take into account. We understand that we represent more than ourselves; we represent our team, our city, our state, sometimes our country. But we also represent our endorsers and our corporate partners and our fans.

When Colin Kaepernick takes a stand against police brutality by kneeling during the national anthem, the public does not completely grasp the risks he is taking in doing so. When the San Francisco 49ers safety Eric Reid takes a knee with Kaepernick during the anthem before a game, he is taking a huge financial and social risk. When the New York Liberty guard Brittany Boyd arrives for the first WNBA playoff game of her career wearing Kaepernick's number 7 jersey, and then does not stand for the anthem, she is taking a monumental risk. When the Phoenix Mercury players Mistie Bass and Kelsey Bone kneel through the anthem, or when the entire WNBA Indiana Fever team kneels and locks arms during the anthem, the public does not fully understand the wide-ranging consequences of their actions. They can and have faced fines and suspensions. When the Seattle Reign star Megan Rapinoe or the Denver Broncos linebacker Brandon Markeith Marshall takes a knee during the anthem, they risk losing millions of dollars in endorsement deals and even face a fierce fan and media backlash. Despite this, the list of sports stars supporting Kaepernick's protest continues to grow.[2]

As professional athletes and sports figures, so much of what we do is in the public eye. Even what is considered our personal choices have public repercussions. Decisions we make about how we look, how we want to live, whom we choose to love, and the causes we support affect us publicly because our decisions play out in a very public way and influence how our fans perceive us—whether this perception is correct or not.

The New York Giants wide receiver Brandon Tyrone Marshall knew he would be fined by the NFL when he decided to raise awareness for mental health issues. In 2011, after being diagnosed with borderline personality disorder (BPD), a mental disorder characterized by unstable moods, Marshall decided to speak out about it despite the social stigma associated with mental health issues, especially for men. When the Green Bay Packers quarterback Aaron Rodgers advocates to bring awareness to the Congo and the conflict diamonds that are mined there, he is fully aware of the possible ramifications of his activism and the potential backlash.

At 6'8" and 207 pounds with an arm span of 7'4", the Phoenix Mercury center Brittney Griner possesses a gender-bending androgynous beauty and graceful ball play that make her a powerful symbol of sexual activism. Formidable on the court, Griner is also true to herself and her sexual identity as she advocates for gender equality, simply by being herself, comfortable in her own skin, regardless of societal expectations of what women should look like. She is the only NCAA basketball player to score 2,000 points and block 500 shots.

A three-time All-American, and a member of the 2016 women's Olympic basketball team that brought home the gold, Griner was named the AP Player of the Year and the Most Outstanding Player of the Final Four in 2012. She is only one of the tremendously talented athletes in the WNBA who are redefining not only basketball but also gender roles. Simply seeing players like Griner on the court inspires the next generation of female athletes to know they can be true to themselves and also be successful in their sport.

When we consider athletes like Billie Jean King, Martina Navratilova, or Venus and Serena Williams, we see that their presence on the court, and their being the best athlete in their sport—not just the best female athlete—changed the game and also how the world viewed female athletes. They did this by debunking stereotypes of how women play or *should* play tennis, and how they should look while doing it.

The Williams sisters have been changing the game since they first set foot on a tennis court. Serena Williams's ferocious play and unapologetic style has made her one of the most successful athletes in the world; not the most successful "female" athlete in the world. Venus Williams has championed equal pay for all women since 1998, and she helped win equal prize money for female tennis players in 2007. At Wimbledon, women had competed for less prize money than their male counterparts ever since they began participating in 1880. By speaking out for equal prize money for women, Venus Williams, with support from other prominent tennis players such as Serena Williams, Jennifer Capriati, Maria Sharapova, Kim Clijsters, and Petra Kvitova, was able to win equal pay for female players, forever altering the landscape of women's tennis.

Despite substantial fines, corporate and sponsor pushback, losing large endorsement deals, public recourse, social stigma, and fan backlash, athletes and sports stars continue to use their unique platform to advocate for change. Before the 2014 Olympics over a dozen athletes publicly spoke out against the Russian law targeting LGBT citizens. The law resulted in a surge of hate crime and numerous arrests of LGBT people in Russia and has been widely referred to in the media as one of the worst human rights violations in the post-Soviet era.

Some sports figures could lose much more than money, endorsements, or fans when they take a stand. At Wimbledon in 2002, Aisam-Ul-Haq Qureshi, a Pakistani Muslim, and Amir Hadad, an Israeli Jew, took the same side in the men's doubles draw knowing they would be going home to their divided nations and facing what could be detrimental fallout from their actions.

In *Ways of Grace*, I explore the many ways that athletes are giving back, taking a stand, and changing the world in far-reaching ways. Sports figures have been championing causes for as long as we have had organized sports. Many were accidental activists, inciting change simply by participating—the boxing icon Muhammad Ali, the baseball legend Jackie Robinson, the tennis superstars Althea Gibson, Billie Jean King, and Martina Navratilova. Merely seeing them perform was powerful enough to change perspectives about their gender or race. Simply by being in the game, these activists fought against oppression, discrimination, inequality, and bias, in whatever form they might take.

Every step forward, no matter how small, every advance in sports to end discrimination and inequality, was a step that brought us closer to the freedoms we all have today. These early accidental activists were not trying to change history; they wanted only to do their best to represent themselves, their race, their gender, and their beliefs, and be allowed all the freedoms they were due. It is their early activism that started and ultimately changed the discourse of human rights and equality. They were the start of the evolution of the sports figure as an advocate for change. I'm buoyed and bolstered by their advancements, by their grit, determination, and drive during a time when simply being on the field, the court, the track, or the baseball diamond brought harassment and threats. The actions of these early forerunners have afforded us many of the civil rights and civil liberties we have today.

Today, the stakes may not be as high politically and socially as they were in the past, but the corporate, media, and fan backlash in professional sports pose their own set of high-stakes risks and ramifications. Despite this, more athletes are taking a stand by publicly speaking out, or quietly advocating for equality or change—regardless of the sometimes harsh financial and social consequences—than at any other time in recent history. And today's activists are starting earlier, as collegiate athletes are seeing their athletic heroes taking a stand on issues of social justice.

In November 2016, the *New York Times* interviewed Nigel Hayes, Jordan Hill, and Bronson Koenig of the University of Wisconsin basketball team, the Badgers. These three talented and outspoken young men want their voice heard on political and social issues even though they are just starting out as athletes and may have trouble getting signed professionally because of it.

Hayes and Hill, both black, took a step away from their teammates during the national anthem before their season-opening game. According to the 2016 article in the *New York Times*,

> Hayes, a senior who was named the preseason Big Ten player of the year, has lobbied for players to be paid, serving as a plaintiff in a lawsuit seeking a freer market for top athletes. . . . Hayes has also posted about the Black Lives Matter movement to his more than 80,000 Twitter followers and recently joined other Wisconsin athletes in demanding university action after a fan appeared in a mask of President Obama and a noose at a Badgers home football game. Hill, a redshirt junior, also writes provocatively on Twitter. And in September, Wisconsin's starting point guard, the senior Bronson Koenig, traveled to support protesters of the Dakota Access pipeline, many of whom are, like him, Native American.[3]

In response to being asked why he was speaking up when it could affect his draft stock, Hayes replied, "At the end of the day, the quote I hang my hat on is, I was black before I picked up a basketball, and when I retire, I'll still be black."

I am proud to take a stand with my fellow athletes and to bring awareness to a cause I believe in. As angry as I am about my incident with the NYPD, that anger is not what made me understand that I had to give voice to it and raise awareness of much-needed protocols between the public and law enforcement. I could not help but wonder how often a situation like mine had played out. When it's your word against five officers, even if the truth is on your side, those odds are hard to deny. I respect our police officers and understand that they put their lives on the line every day to protect and to serve, but the incident left me wondering: To protect and to serve whom?

Law enforcement, not unlike any other organization, is composed of many different types of people with vastly different personalities and points of view. There will always be a few bad apples, spoiling the rest of the bunch. I don't think for a moment that those officers are representative of the entire police force. That the officers in my case made a decision to stand together to protect each other could be indicative of a shared mind-set and an attitude that should have no place in the police department. I'm hoping that bringing awareness to my experience will be a catalyst to start a dialogue about law enforcement and how our officers—our public servants—police us. I am hoping it can start a discussion about creating more checks and balances, protocols that protect our officers and also the public they serve.

In January 2017, the US Justice Department conducted a

thirteen-month investigation into the Chicago Police Department and found that "excessive force was rampant, rarely challenged and chiefly aimed at African-Americans and Latinos."[4] The headline of the 2017 *New York Times* article about the investigation read "Chicago Police Routinely Trampled on Civil Rights, Justice Dept. Says." The article reported that "a blistering report by the Justice Department described far-reaching failures throughout the Chicago Police Department."

During trials for wrongful death, police misconduct, or excessive force, having an independent, unbiased special prosecutor is crucial. Because of the unsettling Justice Department findings of discriminatory law enforcement practices, every police department in the country should require all of its officers to undergo annual diversity, sensitivity, and bias training.

The Kirwan Institute for the Study of Race and Ethnicity at Ohio State University defines implicit bias as "the implicit associations we harbor in our subconscious[, which] cause us to have feelings and attitudes about other people based on characteristics such as race, ethnicity, age, and appearance. These associations develop over the course of a lifetime beginning at a very early age through exposure to direct and indirect messages. In addition to early life experiences, the media and news programming are often-cited origins of implicit associations."

It is crucial that our police officers think twice before using excessive deadly force in their interactions with the public. We must train them to be sensitive, unbiased, concerned, and nonjudgmental when interacting with people in the communities they serve. If not, we must put in place oversight and accountability, because right now there is no real incentive for officers with a history of misconduct or excessive force to change how they interact with the public.

It is also just as imperative for me to take something positive out of my experience, to create something uplifting and affirmative from it. I don't want to ask "Why me?" Instead, I want to use what I have, to incite change in myself, and in the world, in any way I can. That's what I learned from Arthur Ashe. He taught me that in a good situation, you try to help others. In a bad situation, you try to find a way to make it better. There's always going to be someone who is less fortunate. You can find a way to help them, and in so doing you will help yourself and the world. Hopefully you will even inspire others to do the same.

My perception of the world was changed irrevocably that sunny September afternoon I stood outside my hotel. What has also changed is my perception that there is nothing I can do to prevent the indignity of what happened to me from happening to someone else. The best way for me to do that is to continue on the path carved out by my predecessors and stand shoulder to shoulder with my colleagues, to use my voice and my platform to advocate for change, even in the smallest way. To that end, I am going to use what I have, to do what I can.

EARLY TRAILBLAZERS

Accidental Activists

Issues of race, inequity, inequality, and civil rights dominated the headlines in 2016. The start of the Black Lives
Matter movement, social protest against police brutality,
and the polarizing racial and religious rhetoric that reached a
tipping point after the 2016 presidential election placed us at
a crossroads in American history. Subsequent divisive policies
that affect education, health care, gender equality, immigration, and religious freedoms also emerged as dividing issues.
In response, athletes across the country were compelled to use
their voices to engage with the public to raise awareness of
and advocate for social change.

[In the final months of 2016, there was a rise in sports activism in society, and the role of athletes in regard to activism
and social justice has changed drastically within the last year.]]

Their role is particularly pivotal today. We have seen historically how athletics have intersected with change and activism, particularly during integration, the fight for gender equality, and marriage equality. We know that athletes have been able to create and incite change in a way that resonates and has positive impact.

Sports and the sports community do not exist outside the broader context of society. Some of the social issues that affect society have also affected sports; for instance, racial bias, gender inequality, and homophobia. When athletes speak to these things, they speak from a position of authenticity, because these issues affect them as well. When we think back to Muhammad Ali, John Carlos, and Tommie Smith, they understood what was going on in society because it affected them. When they used their platform and their voice, they were not speaking out about something that they did not understand or could not relate to.

In the face of today's social divisiveness, we are seeing the advent of what has been called the accidental activist. However, athletes inciting change has been around since athletes started integrating sports and women began their fight for equal rights. Historically, in professional sports, and in almost no other arena to the same extent, athletes and sports stars have publicly broken racial and gender barriers, at times simply by being in the game. As long as sports have been played, issues of discrimination and inequality have played a part and the athlete has found him- or herself in a public position to take a stand (or not) and start a discourse about inclusion and equality.

Many of us are familiar with the well-known trailblazers like

Jackie Robinson, and even a few of the less well-known "firsts" like the baseball players Fleet and his brother Welday Walker, or the football players Kenny Washington and Woody Strode. Yet when we think about the women who fought for equality and changed how female athletes were viewed in sports—which at the time were geared to and run by men—usually only a few names come to mind, like the tennis legends Althea Gibson and Billie Jean King. There were many others who are not as well known but were just as instrumental in fighting for women's inclusion and representation in sports. Gertrude Ederle was the first woman to swim the English Channel, Shirley Muldowney was known as "the First Woman of Drag Racing." Babe Zaharias was one of the preeminent female athletes of the twentieth century and dominated in several sports. A three-time Olympic gold medalist, Zaharias was an all-around athlete who competed in basketball, golf, tennis, billiards, diving, and bowling. Julie Krone, the winningest female jockey of all time, was the first woman to compete in the Breeders' Cup, and the only female jockey to win a Triple Crown.

These early trailblazers were accidental activists who incited change simply by competing in their sport and being damn good at it, regardless of the color of their skin, their religious affiliation, or their gender. They changed the hearts and minds of America at a time when not only sports but the world was divided by race and gender. To understand the evolution of activism in sports, we have to go back to the beginning, to a time not so long ago when athletes were not consciously trying to change society. Rather, they were simply seeking equitable treatment and opportunities in the sport they loved to play— but in so doing they ended up changing history.

Alife is not important except in the impact it has on other lives." Jackie Robinson lived by his words when he publicly broke Major League Baseball's color barrier in 1947. He opened the doors to players of color in the majors. Each year on April 15, every team celebrates Jackie Robinson Day in honor of his contribution to the sport. Robinson is a particular hero to me. I was a Jackie Robinson scholar for the two years I was in college, from 1997 to 1999. It was so inspirational when all the scholars got together once a year in New York. They were all so impressive and had different experiences at universities all across the country, which they shared. It was invaluable to hear their stories and realize the similarities and the fact that there was still diversity among the scholars and attendees. Jackie Robinson's widow, Rachel Robinson, an esteemed activist in her own right, was always a part of those weekends, and she was as graceful and full of wisdom as you would expect from the life she has led.

Even before Jackie Robinson broke the color barrier, he was an activist for equality. In 1944 Robinson was arrested and court-martialed during training in the army for refusing to move to the back of a segregated bus. He was eventually acquitted of the charges and received an honorable discharge.

Robinson joined the Kansas City Monarchs as a part of the Negro Leagues and played second base until the Brooklyn Dodgers' general manager, Branch Rickey, decided he wanted to integrate baseball. Rickey wanted Robinson not only for his talent, but also because of his behavior on and off the field. Robinson did not drink or smoke, and he'd married his high school sweetheart, Rachel. He was also a calm and focused man and baseball player. Rickey knew Robinson would have a tough time playing during the Jim Crow era, but he believed he could handle it without becoming unnerved or distracted on the field.

Rickey was right: there was a lot to handle on the field as a black player in the 1940s. Robinson endured threats from spectators and from his teammates. The players who taunted him were not reprimanded, nor did they face suspension or punishment. That was just one of the many double standards that players who integrated sports faced. Though Robinson was scorned by some of his teammates and openly harassed by opposing players, he never lost his temper or his focus. To be able to play baseball at that time, he had to practice restraint. Had he retaliated or done anything divisive or unsportsman-like in his first year or two, the consequences could have been extremely severe for him. Instead, he endured the taunts with dignity and grace as he made history.

In 1945 after leaving the Monarchs, Robinson joined the Montreal Royals, which at the time was the Dodgers' top minor-league team. The Royals were not disappointed. In 1946, led by Robinson, attendance at the Royals' games almost tripled over that of the previous year. Over a million people came to watch him perform that year, an amazing number for the minor leagues at the time.

In 1947 Robinson was promoted to the Dodgers and made his Major League entrance on April 15. His was the most eagerly anticipated and dreaded debut in the history of the sport. It represented to blacks and whites the hope and the fear of equality. Robinson's stepping out on the field that day forever changed the complexion of the game. At the end of his first season, Robinson was named the Rookie of the Year. He was named the National League MVP just two years later, in 1949. The Dodgers won six league pennants and one World Series in Robinson's ten seasons, but his contributions extended far beyond the field and still resonate today.

Jackie Robinson is perhaps the most historically significant baseball player ever, ranking with Babe Ruth in terms of his impact on the national pastime. Ruth may have changed the way baseball was played, but Jackie Robinson changed who Americans thought should play. A man of many firsts, Robinson was also the first black player to be inducted into the Baseball Hall of Fame.

Historically, to be an accidental activist is to strive to be great at something and then to be thrust into a social conflict. For me, accidental activism has taken a different form in the sense that today, as athletes, we find ourselves in situations that we did not anticipate. Then, as we go through it, we realize that our voice can make a difference.

Jackie Robinson knew what he was up against when he accepted Rickey's invitation to play in the majors. When I had my incident in New York I had no idea that I would become a national spokesperson against the use of excessive police force. The same with Colin Kaepernick, who before the start of this season, after witnessing another "innocent" person videotaped being killed by law enforcement, decided to use his voice and platform to draw attention to an issue that deeply affected him and also a large segment of the country. I am sure he had no idea how polarizing his protest would be. Many athletes realize that we have a platform that others do not have, but we also realize that we have an obligation to use it.

Many fans know of Robinson's contributions, but he was not the first African American to play in the majors. A less well-known baseball player changed the game *before* Jackie Robinson electrified the baseball field, sparking both awe and anger. Moses Fleetwood Walker, often called Fleet, was really the first African American to play Major League Baseball, in the nineteenth century. In 1884, the Toledo Blue Stockings had two black players—catcher Fleet Walker and his brother, Welday, an outfielder. That year, the Blue Stockings moved from the minor- to the major-league level when they joined the American Association. On May 1, Fleet played against the Louisville Eclipse, and officially broke the color barrier of Major League Baseball.

Between May 1 and September 4, Fleet played forty-two games for Toledo. However, he did not get the opportunity to show what he could do on the field before being taken off the team due to racism. Welday appeared in only five games with Toledo, and Fleet had one of the highest averages on the team.

Both Walker brothers were outspoken about equality and at times brought lawsuits against businesses that discriminated against blacks. In 1888, Welday wrote a letter to *Sporting Life*, decrying discriminatory treatment in the Tri-State League. His letter, published in the March 14 issue, was addressed to the league's president, a Mr. McDermitt:

Sir: I take the liberty of addressing you because noticing in The Sporting Life that the 'law permitting colored men to sign was repealed, etc.' . . . I concluded to drop you a few lines. . . . It is not because I was reserved and have been denied making my bread and butter with some club that I speak. . . . There should be some broader cause—such as want of ability, behavior and intelligence—for barring a player than his color . . . ability and intelligence should be recognized first and last.

Jackie Robinson suffered through terrible harassment while playing baseball. But it barely compares with what Fleet Walker suffered during the one season he played with the Blue Stockings. Walker endured shouted insults on the field and racial discrimination off it. One of Walker's teammates with the Blue Stockings, a pitcher named Tony Mullane, stated that Walker "was the best catcher I ever worked with, but I disliked a Negro and whenever I had to pitch to him I used to pitch anything I wanted without looking at his signals." Despite being an asset to his team, he found it not uncommon for his teammates to not throw the ball to him or include him in the game, which only hurt the Blue Stockings. After Welday and Fleet Walker played their last games for Toledo, no other African American would play in the major leagues until Jackie Robinson, sixty-three years later.

Well-known professional football teams didn't have any black players until 1946, when Kenny Washington and Woody Strode, friends and teammates, played for the Los Angeles Rams, and Marion Motley and Bill Willis played for the Cleveland Browns, Motley as a fullback and linebacker. A versatile athlete, Motley dominated on both offense and defense. He was a well-rounded player who was large but also quick on his feet. Fellow Hall of Fame running back Joe Perry once called Motley "the greatest all-around football player there ever was." A trailblazer, Motley was one of the first African Americans to play the professional game in the modern era.

Frederick Douglass "Fritz" Pollard played in 1920 for the Akron Pros. Pollard was named after the abolitionist Frederick Douglass, who was born a slave. Pollard played in the NFL when it was still called the American Professional Football Association (APFA). Along with Bobby Marshall, Pollard was one of the first two African American players in the NFL in 1920. Pollard also served in World War I. As a star athlete at Brown University, Pollard became, in 1916, the first African American ever to play in the Rose Bowl. He later led the Akron Pros to the APFA championship in 1920. In 1921, while still a running back, Pollard became the co–head coach of the Pros. The following year, he became the first African American coach in the league.

Strode, Washington, and Jackie Robinson (a truly versatile athlete) were all backfield players for the UCLA Bruins in 1939. At this time, neither the league nor the fans were ready for integration, and these trailblazers were heckled and taunted as soon as they hit the field. Washington was also a decathlete who enlisted in the army air corps during World War II and later became an actor. In 1960 he was nominated for a Golden Globe for Best Supporting Actor for his role in *Spartacus*.

The first black player drafted by an NBA team was Chuck Cooper, picked by the Boston Celtics in the 1950 draft. The Washington Capitols chose Earl Lloyd of West Virginia State. At about the same time, the New York Knicks signed Nat "Sweetwater" Clifton from the Harlem Globetrotters. Lloyd made his debut on October 31, 1950, becoming the first African American to play in an NBA game. Cooper made his debut a day later. Clifton, the first to sign a contract, played his first game on November 4, 1950.

These trailblazers became activists by integrating their sport. Their battle beyond being allowed into the major leagues was then to change the hearts and minds of the fans, the members of the rival teams, and, quite often, their own teammates. Being able to focus on your game and getting support from your teammates and fans is as instrumental to an athlete as being in top form to play. I cannot imagine the type of determination, drive, and will to succeed that these stellar athletes had to have had during the early years of integrating sports. Well known or not, they all bore the burden of creating inclusion while changing history along the way.

Let Us in the Game

Now that I have two wonderfully precocious daughters, I am more aware than ever of issues affecting women in society and sports. I look back in appreciation at the monumental women who made themselves a part of the sport they were passionate about and through their perseverance and undeniable talent simply could not be ignored.

There are so many amazingly talented and inspirational women in history who have opened up their sport and changed how women were viewed, and also how girls themselves viewed sports and their place in it. Many of these trailblazers have gone without substantial recognition for their accomplishments during a time in American history when a woman was not even allowed to keep her job if she was pregnant, and when a woman could not get a credit card, have a legal abortion, file a sexual harassment suit, or even refuse to have sex with her husband. Women did not have any of these rights before 1970.

Mildred Ella "Babe" Didrikson Zaharias was born in 1911. A woman ahead of her time, she was considered an all-around athlete of the twentieth century. A natural athlete from a young age, Zaharias competed in a wide range of sports and did phenomenally well in all of them. After dropping out of high school to become an athlete, she ran track and field and won multiple Amateur Athletic Union (AAU) wins and Olympic gold and silver medals in running, jumping, and throwing contests in the 1932 Los Angeles Olympics. Zaharias played All-American basketball and had multiple golf wins—an incredible eighty-two amateur and professional tournaments—and was the first woman to qualify for the Los Angeles Open and play in the PGA Tour. She also played competitive billiards, and competed in sports like tennis, diving, and bowling. In her spare time, she sang and played harmonica, and even recorded several songs on the Mercury Records label. Zaharias faced sexism and jabs from reporters who did not believe that women should be allowed to play sports. Zaharias silenced them by continuing to be one of the best athletes of her time, regardless of her gender or their opinions.

At a time when women struggled for equal rights, Zaharias's goal was to be "the greatest athlete who ever lived." Not the greatest *female* athlete. The greatest athlete. Period. She took on every sport she was allowed to play and excelled at all of them. Her versatility, drive, and all-around natural talent and accomplishments helped chip away at the preconceived notions, prejudices, and institutional barriers facing female athletes in the 1900s.

Gertrude Ederle was born in 1905 and first achieved fame when she competed in the 1924 Olympics. At nineteen, she became the first woman to swim the English Channel and the sixth person in history to achieve that feat. She completed her swim on her second attempt in fourteen hours and thirty-one minutes, beating the record set by the previous male channel swimmers. Her accomplishments may not seem monumental until you consider that she rose to fame in 1920s Manhattan. This was a time when women had to fight for the right to remove their stockings when swimming, because their bare legs might prove distracting.

On her return to New York she was met by a ticker tape parade and a crowd that greeted her arrival at City Hall, where Mayor Jimmy Walker congratulated her. Her achievement earned her the nickname "America's Best Girl" from President Calvin Coolidge, who also invited her to the White House. At that time, her popularity was on par with that of Babe Ruth. By the time Ederle broke the record, women had been allowed to compete in competitive swimming events for only ten years, beginning in 1914. Her record remained unbroken until 1950.

Shirley "Cha Cha" Muldowney was born in 1940 and as the first female member of the Auto Racing All-American team, she was considered the first lady of professional drag racing. Muldowney was a multiple National Hot Rod Association (NHRA) winner, the first person to win the NHRA Winston competition three times. Muldowney was not just a good female racer. Though she was the first woman to accomplish many feats in the sport, many of her records stand for the sport as a whole. This makes her one of the most successful drag racers in history, regardless of gender.

As a young woman, Muldowney was no tomboy; she preferred wearing makeup and pretty dresses to sports. In 1956, at age sixteen, she married Jack Muldowney, a drag racer and mechanic who taught her how to drive. After going to races with her husband, she became intrigued with the racing world, and with Jack's help she learned all about drag racing as well as about the technical aspects and maintenance of the high-performance vehicles. Enamored with racing, Muldowney asked her husband for permission to race. He not only gave it, but he also gave her her first car—a 1940 Ford with a V-8 engine. Muldowney started proving herself in amateur races. When she wanted to go pro, racing's sanctioning bodies, including the NHRA and the American Hot Rod Association (AHRA), were hesitant to grant a woman professional status. Undeterred, Muldowney rallied fellow female racers Judi Boertman, Paula Murphy, and Della Woods, and launched a campaign to be allowed to race professionally. In 1965, she became the first woman pro dragster racer.

Julieann Louise "Julie" Krone was born in 1963, and though you may never have heard of her, she was the winningest female jockey of all time. With 3,456 career wins over eighteen years, Krone was also the first woman to compete in the Breeders' Cup, and as of 2017, she remains the only female jockey to have won a Triple Crown race.

Raised on a horse farm, Krone began riding horses at two and won her first horse show when she was five years old. At the age of fourteen, after watching eighteen-year-old Steve Cauthen win a Triple Crown race, she decided that she wanted to become a jockey. She was a natural rider and although only 4'10", she was a fierce competitor in a sport that saw few female competitors. Male riders tried to sabotage her during races by boxing her horse in by the rail. But Krone fought back. According to a 1988 article in the *Los Angeles Times*, "In 1986, Krone had a similar scuffle with jockey Miguel Rujano at Monmouth Park. Rujano felt that Krone was riding her mount too close to his, and, in order, this developed: Rujano hit Krone in the back of the head with his whip. Krone punched Rujano after the race. Rujano dunked Krone in the jockeys' swimming pool. Krone threw a chair at Rujano."[1]

Despite being a woman in a sport of men who colluded against her, Krone had monumental achievements in the eighties and nineties. She won six races *in one day* at both the Meadowlands and Monmouth Park, and she won five races *in one day* at Saratoga Springs and Santa Anita Park. A truly phenomenal athlete, she became the first woman to be inducted into the National Museum of Racing's Hall of Fame, in 2000.

It is because of trailblazers like these that we have so many of the civil liberties and rights we have today. It is because of them that I have the opportunity, as the son of a black father and a white mother, not only to have played sports professionally, but now to be able to work as a sports commentator and discuss tennis at the games and in the media. These women and men, and so many others like them, heralded equality by their prowess. Their hard-won progress has afforded Americans unalienable rights, regardless of gender, race, sexual orientation, or religion. These phenomenal men and women showcased their amazing talent and fortitude and brought spectators, black and white, men and women, to their feet in recognition of their talent, grit, and strength of character.

Activism Stories:
Big and Small Moments

In 1968 the Mexico City Summer Olympics would sorely test the 5,516 athletes, representing 112 countries in 172 events. According to Olympic.org, "The choice of Mexico City was a controversial one because of the city's high altitude, 2,300m. The altitude proved an advantage in explosive events such as short-distance running, jumping, throwing and weightlifting. But the rarefied air proved disastrous for those competing in endurance events."[2]

On October 16, eight men took their marks on the track for the men's 200-meter dash. The short-distance runners Tommie Smith and John Carlos finished first and third. Smith set a new world record that day of 19.83 seconds. The crowd's exuberance for the exciting race quickly turned to anger when during the medal ceremony, Carlos and Smith walked out in their socks with their heads lowered, and their hands behind their backs, holding their sneakers. They then stood barefoot on the podium, in the gold and bronze positions, to symbolize the poverty and inequality that plagued so many black Americans. Carlos and Smith faced the flags, then bowed their heads and raised their fists while "The Star-Spangled Banner" played.

This gesture was to show support for human rights and equality and to take a stand for civil liberties in a devastating year of tragedies that included the assassination of Martin

Luther King Jr. and Bobby Kennedy. The next day, the International Olympic Committee made Smith and Carlos forfeit their medals. The athletes were suspended from the American team and told to leave the Olympic Village and Mexico immediately. The committee even threatened to boot the entire American team as punishment if they did not leave.

Although their gesture was often called a "Black Power" salute, in his autobiography, *Silent Gesture*, Smith wrote that it was instead a "human rights salute." That expression is regarded as one of the most overtly political statements in the history of the Olympics. The fierce backlash from their protest followed them for decades. Even after the athletes had been disciplined, the repercussions of their actions continued. On October 25, 1968, *Time* magazine wrote: "'Faster, Higher, Stronger' is the motto of the Olympic Games. 'Angrier, nastier, uglier' better describes the scene in Mexico City last week." Back in the States, both Smith and Carlos were criticized in the media and ostracized in the sports community. Smith was discharged from the army. In college, Smith was married with a young son. Someone threw a rock through a glass window at his son's crib, missing the sleeping baby by inches. For years after, Carlos and Smith received death threats and threatening phone calls and notes that read, "Go back to Africa."

It would not be a stretch to see a parallel between the gesture Carlos and Smith made and Kaepernick's gesture. Demonstrating for human rights in a peaceful way does not seem so controversial. Carlos and Smith raised their fists. They did not harm anyone; they did not shout obscenities. It would be a difficult argument to make that their advocating for human rights was not valid or worthwhile. In a similar way, Kaepernick is fighting some of the same battles that were fought in 1968. He is peacefully advocating for human rights. It is not what Kaepernick is protesting that has drawn the fans' and the media's ire, but how he is doing it. It was much the same for Carlos and Smith. Their fight for human rights is one we can all understand and support. It was important to make their stand using the Olympics as their international platform. They decided that for the greatest impact, the world stage would afford them a lasting impression. They were right. Carlos and Smith are now considered heroes fifty years later. I wonder how long it may take for Colin Kaepernick.

John Carlos and Tommie Smith represent the ideal of the athlete activist because they were on top of the world as Olympic medalists, but they decided instead to selflessly use their platform to incite change. They were shunned for using their public moment on the podium to bring awareness to what they saw as inequality in their sport and in America. They wanted to show their displeasure with a system that they felt did not treat all men fairly or equally. Because of this dedication to their cause, they lost it all in an instant. Their peaceful protest had a ruinous ripple effect that lasted for decades.

I cannot imagine that they knew beforehand the impact it would have on their personal and professional lives. In addition to threats and harassment, they lost sponsorships and endorsements, and ultimately ruined any chances to compete at the international level ever again. Yet the fact that they made such a life-changing decision during what could be seen as one of the most important moments in their lives represents a monumental sacrifice. Although they were excoriated in the media for being selfish, that act was one of the most selfless choices I could imagine anyone making as an athlete. That gesture, in that moment, had such a negative effect on their lives, but it inspired change in a positive way simply by raising awareness at a time when the world was watching. This is one of the few times I think using the word "hero" to describe an athlete is apt. Having athletic prowess and honing that skill for most of your life is impressive and admirable, but standing up for others who do not have a voice when you can—that makes you heroic.

Today Carlos and Smith are hailed for their contribution to civil rights. They received the Arthur Ashe Courage Award at the 2008 ESPYs, and there is a statue erected in their honor at San Jose State University. However, also standing on the podium was a third man, whose story and selfless, unwavering support of their protest has all but disappeared from the annals of history. A white Australian, Peter Norman, the silver winner, who came from behind Carlos to overtake him for second place by inches, set a record at 20.06 seconds, which is still an Australian record.

Norman knew what Smith and Carlos intended to do. After winning the first, second, and third positions in the 200-meter race, the three men stood in the stadium tunnel waiting for the medal ceremony. Smith and Carlos, each wearing a black glove on one hand, discussed their now-historic plan. Norman, standing not far away, asked what they were talking about. Carlos turned to him and said, "Do you believe in human rights?" Without pausing, Norman said, "Of course." Carlos told him that he and Smith intended to stand on the podium wearing badges in support of human rights and equality. Carlos held out the Olympic Project for Human

Rights badge they intended to wear during the ceremony and asked if he would wear one. Again without pausing, Norman reached for it and said, "I'll stand with you."

Norman wanted to be included and to give them his full support. As they stood on the podium, the spectators could see the small white badge with a green wreath that all three wore pinned to their chest. Norman knew he could not raise his fist along with them, so he wore the badge as a show of support for human rights and solidarity with the two Americans who would become his lifelong friends. In 2006, when Norman died at age sixty-four from a heart attack, Smith and Carlos were his pallbearers.

From the perspective of many in Norman's home country, his act was not a courageous thing for a white Australian to do; rather, it was thought of as a shameful act. But Norman did not view it that way. He felt it more important to advocate for equality with Smith and Carlos. He paid a steep price for it when he returned to Australia.

Norman kept the badge for the rest of his life, despite the backlash he faced—one that continued until his death. The white badge was an important symbol that tied him to Smith and Carlos, to that critical moment in history, and to his place in it. Norman and the part he played that momentous day to advance human rights was as lasting and powerful as the statement that Smith and Carlos made. Decades later, history would vindicate Smith and Carlos, whose actions are now celebrated, but Norman was never fully accepted back into Australian society or the athletic community.

Norman was inarguably the greatest Australian sprinter, whose time of 20.06 that day in Mexico City was a personal best and an Australian 200-meter record that is still unbroken almost fifty years later. Despite this, Norman, a five-time 200-meter champion, never again competed professionally after Mexico City. In Australia, the Olympic silver winner was ostracized and his family shunned. Norman was reprimanded by Australia's Olympic authorities and then ostracized by the Australian media. Despite his qualifying for both the 100-meter and the 200-meter races, the Australian Olympic track team did not send Norman, or any other sprinters, to the 1972 Munich Summer Olympics. It was the first time in modern Olympic history that no Australian sprinters would participate. Australian officials said that they supported Norman at the 1968 games. Norman represented his country at the 1972 Commonwealth Games.

Norman left the sports world behind, and looked for work, but it was hard to find. The Australian silver medal winner and record holder eventually secured a job as a gym teacher, but he battled depression and alcoholism for many years.

"If we were getting beat up, Peter was facing an entire country and suffering alone," John Carlos said of the man who became his lifelong friend. Norman was reportedly given the opportunity to better his circumstances, but it would mean condemning John Carlos's and Tommie Smith's actions. Had he done so, according to reports, Norman would have secured a stable job through the Australian Olympic Committee and been part of the organization of the 2000 Sydney Olympic Games. Norman, although now in dire financial straits, chose not to speak out against the gesture Smith and Carlos had made, or his part in it.

Subsequently, Norman, the greatest Australian sprinter in

history and the holder of the 200-meter record, was not invited to the Olympics in Sydney. It was the American Olympic Committee that asked him to join its group. Norman died without his country ever fully recognizing him for the hero he was in bringing home the silver medal for the 1968 Olympics or for his stellar athletic accomplishments.

Years later, in 2012, the Australian Parliament considered a posthumous apology to Norman. According to a 2012 article in *The Nation*,

> Here is the text of the resolution that will be offered into parliament by MPs Rob Oakeshott and Andrew Leigh:
>
> That this House; Recognises the extraordinary athletic achievements of the late Peter Norman, who won the silver medal in the 200 metres sprint running at the 1968 Mexico City Olympics, in a time of 20.06 seconds, which still stands as the Australian record;
>
> Acknowledges the bravery of Peter Norman in donning an Olympic Project for Human Rights badge on the podium, in solidarity with African-American athletes Tommie Smith and John Carlos, who gave the black power salute;
>
> Apologises to Peter Norman for the wrong done by Australia in failing to send him to the 1972 Munich Olympics, despite repeatedly qualifying; and Belatedly recognises the powerful role that Peter Norman played in furthering racial equality.[3]

The Australian Olympic Committee has since disputed the claims made in the Australian Parliament apology about

Norman being shunned in supporting Carlos and Smith. According to the November 2015 *Australian Olympic Committee News* article "Peter Norman Not Shunned by AOC," the AOC made the following comments:

AOC: Peter Norman's performance at the Mexico 1968 Olympic Games to win silver in the 200m and then support the black salute from American gold and bronze medallists, Tommie Smith and John Carlos, will forever give him a place in Olympic folklore.

The Australian Team Chef de Mission at the 1968 Games Mr Julius Patching supported Norman and this continued throughout his life including honorary roles at Australian Olympic Committee events.

There is a misleading and inaccurate report on social media that the Australian Olympic Committee shunned Peter Norman.

When the incident happened at the 1968 Mexico Games, Norman was not punished by the Australian Olympic Committee (AOC). He was cautioned by Patching that evening, and then given as many tickets as he wanted to go and watch a hockey match. That was his punishment! This is confirmed in the Official History of the Australian Olympic Movement, compiled by the late and respected historian Harry Gordon.

It has been claimed that Norman was not picked for the next Olympics in 1972 because of the incident in 1968. This too is incorrect. At the time Ron Carter, athletics writer for *The Age*, wrote that Norman was injured and failed to perform at the Trials.

In the lead up to the Sydney 2000 Olympics, Norman was involved in numerous Olympic events in his home city of Melbourne. He announced several teams for the AOC in Melbourne and was on the stage in his Mexico 1968 blazer congratulating athletes. He was very much acknowledged as an Olympian and the AOC valued his contribution.

As for the accusation that Norman was not invited to the Sydney 2000 Olympic Games. The AOC was not in a financial position to invite all Olympians to Sydney 2000. They were given special assistance to purchase tickets but it would have cost the AOC hundreds of thousands of dollars to bring Olympians from around the country to Sydney for the Games. The suggestion he was shunned is totally incorrect. He was treated like any other Australian Olympian.

Norman has been profiled by the AOC over recent years on the AOC corporate website—corporate.olym pics.com.au—as one "Of Our Finest" Olympians.[4]

We can certainly understand why the African Americans Carlos and Smith would want to risk so much to take a stand for human rights and racial equality, but why would Peter Norman, a white man, commit to a cause that may not have directly affected him when he could have simply enjoyed his moment of victory? He could have returned home to Australia a hero, his financial future secure. Perhaps the best answer comes from Norman's own words, in the award-winning 2008 documentary *Salute*, written, directed, and produced by his nephew Matt Norman. *Salute* is an insightful account of that historic moment in civil rights history. It is also a shocking reminder of how the world was less than fifty years ago.

"I couldn't see why a black man couldn't drink the same water from a water fountain, take the same bus, or go to the same school as a white man," Norman says in the film. "There was a social injustice that I couldn't do anything about from where I was, but I certainly hated it. It has been said that sharing my silver medal with that incident on the victory dais detracted from my performance. On the contrary, I have to confess, I was rather proud to be part of it."

All three Olympians should go down in history for putting their principles before their personal interests, and for their willingness to accept the outcome.

Game. Set. Match.

I can think of no other athlete who has had such an all-around impact on so many lives in so many areas of society than Billie Jean King. Being a tennis superstar was only one of her many accomplishments. King stood for the acceptance of people regardless of race, religion, or sexual orientation. She advocated for women's rights, gender equality, LGBT rights, and marriage equality. She also fought for equal pay for female athletes and for equality not only in sports but also in the workforce.

King, who always thought that "if you could see it, you could be it," used her global tennis platform to not only inspire, educate, and empower women—who saw that she was just as good an athlete as men—but also inspire men to see that women were not less than men, but that they were equal. In 1973 King threatened to boycott the US Open unless women were awarded equal prize money as men, and won. Using her leverage as the defending champion, King secured for female champions the same prize purse as the men's champion.

On Mother's Day in 1952, when Billie Jean King was nine years old, she went with her family to Wrigley Field in Los Angeles. As she looked out at the players it dawned on her that there were no women. She was shocked when she found out that women did not play professional baseball, and, in fact, many women did not play professional sports at all. She was disappointed but determined that nothing would keep her from playing tennis, a game that she loved. King eventually saved enough money to buy herself a racket. It was lavender, and she was so thrilled that she slept with it. King was so excited about learning to play that she read all the tennis books she could find at the time, all three. Then she went to the park for her first tennis instruction. At the end of the day, King ran home and told her mother that she found what she wanted to do with her life.

King first learned tennis in the late 1950s on the public courts of her hometown in Long Beach, California. She worked two jobs to pay her way through college. At that time, sports scholarships were not offered to women. It was not until 1972 that Congress enacted the federal civil rights statute known as Title IX of the Education Amendments. This amendment allowed for equality in sports in the United States. Before Title IX, women and girls were not given the same benefits as men and boys in terms of educational opportunities, participation, and federal financial assistance.

What this meant was that any federal funds given to a high school, college, or university, either public or private, had to be given equally to boys and girls. Before Title IX, young women could not get an athletic scholarship in the States. The amendment enabled women to receive sports scholarships. That changed everything. It allowed female athletes the same financial opportunities as male athletes to attend school and focus fully on sports without having to work extra jobs to afford an education, as King did. This meant that women now had the same opportunities as men, and it created equality in education and sports activities. Female athletes could now play team sports in a way they could not before.

Despite the good that Title IX did for female athletes, King believed that you could have a law, but until you changed hearts and minds nothing had really changed at all. She wanted to start that change. King worked hard on her game, perfecting her hard-charging style and aggressive play. By twenty-three she was the top-ranked women's tennis player in the world, having won both the US Open and Wimbledon. King has said many times that she doesn't like tennis, she *loves* it, and that when she plays she feels like she can do anything. She feels freedom, the freedom to do or be whatever she wants.

However, tennis, her love for the game, and her outspokenness for women's rights and equality took her farther than I think even she could have imagined. By the end of the 1960s, King was speaking out against a long-standing—and growing—disparity in the pay and prize money awarded to men and women. In 1968 women won prize money in competitions, but King never thought women would get less prize money than their male counterparts. At Wimbledon that year, women made less than half the prize money that men did. Before King took on the male-dominated tennis establishment, women players made $14.00 a day.

When the male players formed their own union, the Association of Tennis Professionals (ATP), King saw an opportunity. She suggested that the organization also include women, but it rejected her suggestion. She would not be put off. In true King style, she decided that if female tennis players could not be a part of the men's association, she would start an association for women. In 1970, she founded the Women's Tennis Association to unite all of women's tennis in one tour and create tournaments to play for prize money. She started the WTA by getting nine players (the Original Nine) to sign one-dollar contracts to compete in a new women's tour, the Virginia Slims Series. Her dream in creating the association was for every girl, from all over the world, to know that "if she were good enough that there would be a place for them to play, to actually compete and to make a living."

The Battle of the Sexes

There was a lot of skepticism about the women's association and tour. The main argument was that no one would want to pay to watch women play. In 1973, in the midst of King's fight for equal pay and prize money, Bobby Riggs, a former number one player who had won the Triple Crown at Wimbledon (and also a self-proclaimed male chauvinist), issued a challenge to the top female tennis players to try to beat him in a match. Sitting next to King during a news conference, he proclaimed, "There's no way a woman can play tennis with a good man tennis player. This is a battle of the sexes!"

The fifty-year-old Riggs had set his sights on King, but when she declined his challenge, he went after the Australian Margaret Court, the top women's player. At that time, Court, a Grand Slam winner, had three Wimbledon wins and three women's singles wins. When Court accepted, Riggs destroyed her on the court in the first, less publicized Battle of the Sexes match, played on Mother's Day in 1973 and later known as the Mother's Day Massacre. Riggs easily defeated Court from start to finish, leading her two games to love in the first set, and Court never recovered. After that, King felt she had to play Riggs to vindicate female athletes. After she accepted, their match took on a life all its own.

Riggs's challenge, that he could outplay any woman at the time, had started out more as a publicity stunt, but it got King thinking about society and what a match like this could mean to young girls and women. King knew that she had to play him and she knew that she had to win, especially after the loss Court suffered. Unlike Court, who didn't consider herself a women's libber and was playing for herself against Riggs, King, a staunch advocate of women's rights, felt that she was playing for *all* women. And she knew if she won she would put women's tennis on the map. For King it was about much more than tennis; it was about social change, and it fit in perfectly with what was going on in the world at that time, with the women's liberation and feminist movements. News of Riggs and King's match took off in the media like a rocket. The winner would not only take home $100,000 in prize money but would also claim bragging rights in the age-old argument of men versus women. But not only did King have to win, she knew she would have to win big. She would have to run him into the ground.

So she took up the gauntlet, and with the world watching they met across the net on September 20, 1973, in the Houston Astrodome for the highly anticipated and much publicized Battle of the Sexes match. King was determined to win the match that would ultimately define her career. To King, she had to win because not only would it be a win for her, it would be a win for women everywhere. It would be a win for any young girl or woman who was told to believe that she was the weaker sex. It would be a win for any young girl or woman who had been told that she did not have what it took to be a real competitor, and compete on the same level as men. King thought that women were on their way to achieving equality, and she wanted it to continue. But she worried that another loss by a woman to the trash-talking Riggs—who liked to say that King "plays well, for a woman"—could set women back fifty years.

The match started off on a gorgeous sunny day with so much pomp and pageantry that it looked more like a coronation than a tennis match. Cheerleaders in skimpy outfits kicked up their heels as a band played and thousands of fans filed into the stadium. Ninety million people watched the match internationally and fifty million Americans watched at home. Often called colorful and controversial, Bobby Riggs was wheeled into the stadium in a rickshaw surrounded by beautiful women while King entered in a chariot of brightly colored ostrich feathers, pulled by men from the Rice University track team. And although there was a carnival atmosphere in the stadium, underneath it all was a sense of a real battle to prove who was the better sex, men or women.

King, a crusader for women's rights, carried the weight of

all the women watching. She felt an overwhelming sense of responsibility, and many media pundits predicted that she would buckle under the pressure. She proved them wrong. Once the pomp and circumstance was over and the tennis began, King methodically took Riggs apart in what was undeniably an explosive match from beginning to end. King matched Riggs stroke for stroke, even as he hammered her backhand with shot after shot. When King won spectacularly in straight sets, 6–4, 6–3, 6–3, Riggs hopped over the net, shook her hand, and said, "I underestimated you." It was an indescribable moment for King because her father had always told her, "Respect your opponent, never underestimate them."

In a match that captivated the world, played in a packed stadium, King defeated Riggs, and the men and women in the audience rose to their feet in appreciation of her victory. The next day the headlines heralded: "Mrs. King Defeats Riggs. King Wins Battle of the Sexes."

King's victory was twofold. It was a victory for women's rights, and it sparked social change. In that beautiful moment when she beat Riggs, she silenced all the naysayers and doubters who believed that women were not as good as men, or could not compete on the same level. At the same time, she also gave women and young girls across the world the confidence to believe in themselves and to fight for their rights. When she trounced Riggs she started a women's revolution in sports and placed sports squarely at the center of a national debate about gender equality. She gave women confidence and empowerment. But she wasn't finished.

In addition to the WTA, King cofounded World Team Tennis in 1974 with her husband, Larry King. The WTT is a pioneering co-ed tennis league, featuring matches of different configurations of men's and women's single and mixed-doubles teams. Since its inception, the league has drawn top players including King, Bjorn Borg, Chris Evert, John McEnroe, Martina Navratilova, Evonne Goolagong, Andre Agassi, Pete Sampras, Venus and Serena Williams, Lindsay Davenport, and Martina Hingis, to name only a few of the exceptional tennis players who participated. I have been a part of WTT since 1999 and I competed last in 2016.

The mixed-gender format not only highlights the interplay of the phenomenal men and women on the teams but also unifies them as a team instead of separating them by gender. This was something King has fought for her entire professional career. King became commissioner and major owner of the league in 1984, following her retirement from the professional tennis circuit.

King has always said that champions adjust and that pressure is a privilege, which is also the title of her memoir. To her it was a pleasure to have pressure. It meant you were really doing something. Pressure came with the game, and to her it was what you did with it that mattered. She reminded herself over and over that pressure was a privilege the night before her match with Riggs.

King gained all the lessons she needed in life from the tennis court. She called them lessons in life from the court. Every ball that came toward her meant she had to make a decision, she had to be nimble, she had to adjust per volley, she had to think, she had to strategize. Every single decision she made on the court had consequences. King used this same approach in life. She was equal parts emotion and strategy. When she

wanted something emotionally, she strategized a way to make
it happen. When she wanted women to be a part of the men's
tennis organization, and she was denied, she created her own
association. When she wanted to play professionally, but
women were not offered sports scholarships in the sixties, she
worked two jobs to earn enough money to make it a reality.

Years later, in 2009, when President Obama bestowed on
King the Presidential Medal of Freedom, the nation's highest civilian honor, he told her that he saw her historic match
against Riggs when he was twelve years old and it made such a
difference in him, in how he perceived women and what they
were capable of, that it changed the way he would raise his
daughters. This is truly an amazing statement that shows the
impact an activist can have not only in the moment but also on
future generations. No president would ever make such a monumental change, such as how he decided to raise his daughters,
based solely on a tennis game. What affected him was that
King was fighting for social change, as it affected women.

Coming Out on Her Own Terms

In a life rife with personal and career struggles, King cites being outed in 1981 in a palimony suit by her former secretary
Marilyn Barnett, who was suing her for support, as one of
the biggest struggles of her life. The suit forced her out of the
closet, making her the first prominent lesbian in sports history.
She decided to have a press conference and come out to the
world. With her husband, Larry King, and her parents, Betty
and Bill Moffitt, sitting next to her, she announced that she
had indeed had an affair with Marilyn Barnett.

King's coming out was unprecedented. Public figures, sports figures, actors, and politicians simply did not come out as gay in the 1980s. King did not realize she was gay until 1968 at twenty-five, after she had already married her college sweetheart, Larry King, whom she divorced in 1987. When she made her announcement that day in front of a phalanx of cameras and journalists, there was a collective gasp. She thought that the truth would finally set her free. But the backlash was immediate. She lost all her endorsement money within twenty-four hours of the announcement. This did not keep King from continuing to use her global platform to speak out for women's rights, gay rights, and eventually marriage equality.

Today the WTA is the global leader in women's professional sports, with more than 2,500 players representing nearly one hundred nations competing for a record $139 million in prize money. A former world number one professional tennis player, King has won 39 Grand Slam titles, including 12 singles, 16 women's doubles, and 11 mixed-doubles titles. But somehow none of them would prove as memorable as her victory against Bobby Riggs in the Battle of the Sexes. This is in part because it was not only a win for King, it was a win for all women. King's success that day and over the course of her stellar career inarguably paved the way for equality for all female athletes. Because of King, today equal prize money is awarded in all four major tennis tournaments for men and women.

King was not just a pioneer of women's tennis—she also pioneered equal pay for women off the courts. During the course of her life she helped change how women and men perceived feminine identity, women's role in sports, and also the role of sports in social justice. Her match against Bobby Riggs proved that women were equal with men not only on the court, but also off the court, because her victory helped empower women to believe in themselves and their role in society. Because of King's win, women felt empowered in the workforce to ask for a raise. Some women had waited ten or fifteen years to do so. But feeling empowered and on equal footing with men, women asked for raises in jobs they had worked at for years, without equal pay or raises, and many got them.

King fought for equal rights for women because women have historically had fewer rights and freedoms and were also considered less than men. They were considered not as smart, not as strong, not as resourceful. But King knew none of this was true, and it drove her to want to make a difference in women's lives. She wanted to be a voice for those she felt could not speak up for themselves. King's challenge to sexism, the supportive climate of second-wave feminism, and the legislative clout of Title IX sparked a women's sports revolution in the 1970s that fundamentally reshaped American society.

What King did and continues to do as an activist and advocate moved female athletes forward in leaps and bounds and still affects them today. Sadly, there is still work to be done, as US women today earn seventy cents on the dollar to men. Companies employing women in positions of power are still far too rare. It appears that it takes women starting the companies (which, statistically, are more successful than those founded by men) to have their leadership roles filled with women. What King started must continue—we cannot lose the momentum. The sports community is lucky to have athletes like Venus Williams and Megan Rapinoe who are willing to fight and continue fighting for equality for women in sports.

Know Your History

King is vocal about the issues that are important to her and has been since the beginning of her career. I appreciate that she made time to speak with me for this book. I was curious to find out what drove her to be the outspoken advocate she has been and when the first time was that she felt the need to advocate. When I caught up with King I had a long list of questions to ask her. King is one of my tennis heroes. Not only has she been a trailblazing tennis player but she has been an activist throughout her entire forty-year tennis career. First and foremost, I wanted to find out about the first time King decided to advocate, the issue she spoke out about, and what that felt like for her. King didn't have to think long about her answer.

"I had an epiphany when I was twelve," she responded. "I was at the Los Angeles Tennis Corp during the Pacific Southwest where all the top players would go after the US Nationals, which is the US Open now. I had played tennis about a year and I started to understand that tennis is a platform, it could take you places and you could do things with it. But I knew for me as a girl, it would be a different journey than for a boy. There are a lot of similarities between race and gender that people don't pick up on sometimes. I do, because I'm a woman. I'm on the other side, a side that doesn't always do as well. As a man of color, you and I should be hand in hand in a lot of issues that affect our race and gender. Of course, you have daughters now, so you'll start to understand issues of gender through them.

"That was the moment of truth for me, to decide that I

was basically going to fight for equality for the rest of my life. To fight for the same opportunities as men. I didn't know how I was going to do it, and it took me a long time to do it. I really fought for pro tennis, and sometimes that got me in trouble. Those were really difficult days to try to get the game to be professional, and on fourteen dollars a day, women made far less than the men. It really bothered me. Growing up, my sports were team sports; basketball was my favorite. Then I played baseball, softball. I loved track and field. You know, the professional sports. To me, to be a professional always meant you're the best.

"I then get into tennis, my last sport ever, which I didn't know anything about. I fell in love with tennis. I read the history. I learned everything I could. In my mind as I went through my journey, I was always fighting for equality, all types of equality, not only gender equality. When we finally had professional tennis I wanted the men and women to have the same association. The men rejected us. They said no. Plan B was to start a women's professional tennis, which we were lucky to be able to do.

"It was quite a journey, and as you go through those moments, you start to build a platform. As pro athletes, we are very fortunate that we have exposure. It's our job to use it as long as we're careful, thoughtful, and kind. But also tough. It's amazing to have this opportunity. It's a blessing. That's how I feel every day when I wake up. I count my blessings, and think, What can I do today to make the world a better place? If you think that way, you'll notice opportunities to speak up. That was why I played Bobby Riggs. It was no athletic feat to beat him. It was an opportunity for social change.

"Before 1972 there were classroom quotas. For instance, as a woman, if you wanted to go to medical school at Harvard, the quota in the classroom before 1972 for women was five percent. If your daughter wanted to study medicine at Harvard, before 1972, she had a five percent chance of getting in because of the quota. I want to get fifty-fifty all the time, that was our battle. Today it's about fifty-seven percent women. When people who have been oppressed get the doors open, they take advantage of it. It's like breathing. It's like truly breathing the air for the first time. That's what we did with the WTA.

"As I said, when I decided to play Bobby Riggs, it was about social change. It wasn't about tennis. What happened during that match was important on two fronts. One was a chance to change the world's perception of women as athletes, change not only men's perception of women, but also a woman's perception of what she was capable of. The second was we got tennis exposed to the world like never before in the history of our sport. We're a new sport professionally. So the timing for both men's and women's pro tennis was fantastic. That was the explosion of the country's and the world's interest in tennis. It was because of that match. The match was seen by ninety million people worldwide and around forty or fifty million here.

"Within six months, you couldn't get a tennis court. Men in the league never really talk about it. They never bring it up or mention it. Yet it's helped give tennis players and the associations a lot more exposure. That was the reason. It wasn't the pro tours. The pro tours got their first network contracts because of that match as well. No one talks about it in connection to the match. That match really changed the way the world perceived professional tennis. It is the same as speaking out about issues that are important to you. It's not how you perceive it but how the world perceives it. That's what we try to change. At that time it was important how the world perceived it.

"It's no different, James, from what you are doing by speaking out about your incident with the police officer. You are trying to do the right thing and speak out for people of color. What's been happening to young African American boys, is just not right. I remember hearing Hillary's first campaign speech at the David Dinkins event at Columbia. That was her first campaign speech. It was all about the incarceration of young African Americans. It was an amazing speech, discussing what she would do to try to make it better. I thought that as the subject matter for her first campaign speech it was amazing. We have to keep trying to do the right thing, to speak out for people who don't have your voice or platform. I think any time I can speak out, then good. I've had so many opportunities to speak out. But you have to think about what you're doing, not just feel impassioned to do it. You have to be careful emotionally when you become active, because sometimes it takes on a life of its own."

I knew exactly what King meant by "it takes on a life of its own." When I decided to speak to the media about my incident in New York, I had no idea that I might end up where I am today, as an advocate for victims of police misconduct or the author of a book about sports activism. As such, I was curious about how King prepared for her role as an advocate. Every athlete prepares for protest differently. How did she prepare for advocacy—to make a statement or to commit an act of activism? And how should a young athlete go about it, or is it something that just comes naturally? Clearly there is no handbook about activism, yet it's a role that athletes have found themselves in for decades.

"First of all they need to read history," King answered almost immediately. "The more you know about history, the more you know about yourself. I read *Founding Sisters*, for instance. These are the women who sacrificed everything so that women could vote. Then I read books about male gender too, because I like both. My advocacy isn't limited to only one gender. I'm really big on including everyone, men, women. Just trying to get equality in the workplace to be equal. It's the pay, it's the advancement. It's the opportunity, empathy. All the things that are important. It's not only about diversity and inclusion. You can have inclusion if you have diversity, and diversity with no inclusion. For me, it's about equality across the board. In the workplace it starts on the corporate level.

"Of course I fight for girls and women in sports. We founded the Women's Sports Foundation in 1974. We are the guardian angels of Title IX in sports. If you read something about girls in sports it's usually based on our research. We've given out more than eighty million dollars in grants to girls and organizations that empower them. We also do a program with espnW called Sports 4 Life. It offers grants to increase Latinas' and African American girls' participation in sports. They are the ones who are often left behind. If they get into sports they'll do better academically. They'll graduate.

"After I played Bobby Riggs I started the Women's Sports Foundation. I had an opportunity, I had a platform. I had exposure. People knew who I was. I knew Title IX could be weakened over the years. How important it was to vote for it. It's only thirty-seven words, but what it really states is, 'No discrimination based on sex.' Which meant girls can't be discriminated against. If things had been reversed, the boys would have been as behind as the girls were. Whatever the situation may be, it's about equality. Those are the things I care about. Everything I care about is based on equality.

"If you're in collegiate or professional sports, you have an opportunity to stand up and be counted. Make sure you think about how you want to speak out. What's at stake? You have to decide carefully when you do something, because it's with you forever. You have to decide if that's the way you want to express yourself. There's a lot of thought that should go into it. If you don't think it through, your intention won't be clear. For instance, take the Rooney Rule. Even though the intention was one hundred percent good you're not guaranteed how it will be received."

King's point about the Rooney Rule and its intention is an interesting one. The Rooney Rule is named after Dan Rooney, the owner of the Pittsburgh Steelers and the chairman of the league's diversity committee. It was created by the National Football League in 2003 and requires every franchise to interview at least one minority candidate for the head coaching position when there is a vacancy. The rule is clear that a minority candidate must be interviewed for a head coaching position when one opens up. It says nothing, though, about actually having to hire one. This can be considered a loophole. A team can follow the rule by interviewing a minority member for a head coaching position without really considering him as a possible candidate.

I agree with King that the Rooney Rule is well intentioned, and some people believe that there are African American coaches who were able to secure their positions because of the rule. Some people in the football community believe that is how Mike Tomlin got the head coaching position for the Steelers, which is owned by the Rooney family, primarily by Dan Rooney and his son Art II. But I don't believe it has made the difference that it was supposed to or that people hoped it would.

In addition to knowing your history and thinking through your statement or act so your intentions are not misconstrued, did King have any other advice on how to prepare for advocacy or activism? Also, with all the protests in the months before our talk in 2016, has she found any difference today in the activist athlete culture from that in the '70s, when she had her epic match and started on her path to activism?

"Those are the kinds of things I think everyone who wants to create change should think about," King replied. "When I give lectures and talks I always tell the audience that it's about them, it's not about me. It's about their influences on life and on others. And that it's really important to actively listen. When they have the urge or the spirit moves them to speak, you have to be kind, and you have to be careful, but also bold. Think about it, plan it out, and then go for it. When you go for it, you go per volley. I think it really is good if you're calm, thoughtful, and maybe ask others who have spoken out in the past. Think it through. If you have time. Sometimes you don't have time. When I haven't had time to think something through I just go with my truth, whatever it is. Just go with it. As long as I'm trying to be kind and good and thoughtful, and truthful, I figure I'll be okay.

"As for the difference between the activism during my playing years and today, I think the seventies were an amazing time. There were so many things changing, and the movement for women's equality and rights for women was very strong at that time. Women couldn't get a credit card until 1973 without a man cosigning for it. So much has changed since then, clearly. Then there was a gap when athletes were quiet. No one said anything for a while. To me I never felt I knew Michael Jordan and Tiger Woods as human beings. For a while they dominated sports. I always felt that they were on a pursuit of excellence. I can understand that, especially operating at their level athletically. But what did they feel about society? What did they feel about people of color? What did they think? They never talked about their personal take on those things. So I thought there was a big gap there for a while. Today the athletes are much more active, and much more into activism than they've ever been."

I agree with King. Activism since the '70s has changed drastically, because in the '70s there was an activist culture. Then there was definitely a huge gap, particularly during the time Michael Jordan was widely reported to have said, "Republicans buy sneakers too." This quote has been debunked, but it is indicative of the era at that time. That gap could have been because of corporate sponsorship, either fear of losing endorsers or fear of not attracting them. Today there has been a huge surge in sports activism. For instance, LeBron James has advocated on two fronts. He used his voice to endorse Hillary Clinton for president and he also uses his substantial economic resources to create change in communities that need it. And Steph Curry, who had been pretty quiet and low key on the activism front, recently spoke out because he disagreed with Kevin Plank, the Under Armour CEO, who said that Donald Trump was an asset.

Athletes today are more willing to speak up. Social media has also changed our reach. Every athlete has a direct link to his or her fans all the time. This is something athletes did not have on the same level in the '80s or '90s. Also, in those days, the beat reporters in the locker rooms would ask questions specific only to the game just played, not about athletes' points of view of social issues, which we're seeing more of today. So the fans did not get to know them in those days. As Billie Jean King said, fans didn't know Michael Jordan or Tiger Woods, we didn't know how they felt about society. Today, you can find out such information through the 24/7 news cycle or from social media. There is so much more the professional athlete can talk about. We all have a point of view. Today we are able to learn about athletes on a more personal level, about their personalities and their perspective on society. Did King think there was more athletes could be doing today to spark change, and if so, what? And should athletes feel a responsibility to be involved in advocacy and activism? Is this a role we can and should take on? King didn't need to pause for her answer.

"Yes, I do believe that athletes are in a position to create change. With the money and the wealth today's athletes have, they can take more chances now. More risk as well. It's not like when I was making fourteen dollars a day. And even then I was almost suspended. The Original Nine who started women's professional tennis—we were threatened that we'd never get to play again. So when you're making no money, that's one thing, but at the levels so many of these athletes are playing at today it is a lot tougher. I've always loved LeBron because he speaks out. He loves Cleveland and has tried to improve his community. He's very different from Michael Jordan. He's gonna make a big difference in the world. To me it's always been much more important what I did off the court, than what I did on. I always wanted to be a force off the court. That's what matters most to me in my life.

"To answer your first question, James, about what really started me on a path to activism, it still goes back to when I was twelve years old. My brother, Randy, and I were talking the other day, and we realized that growing up we were the watchers on the block. If we ever saw bullying he and I would step in. I started to wonder why we were like that. Why did we want to speak up for or protect people? Then the answer occurred to me. My dad was a firefighter. He would run into a burning building when everybody else was running out of it. More firefighters die than police officers, which a lot of people don't know. It got me thinking about the exposure I had as a child. Every day he left for work, I knew he might not come back. You think about those things as a child. You're influenced by them. Even if you're not aware of it. I think that taught us to do the right thing, to always try to do the right thing. Everyone has to do it their own way. You just do the best you can."

CHANGING THE GAME

The Unifying Power of Sports

The reason why athletes have been such powerful advocates for social justice and change is because sports is universal. It cuts across racial, economic, and religious strata in society. It is one of the reasons athletes have traditionally been successful when they decide to take a stand or use their platform. Most people enjoy sports, in one form or another. Sports is something that people get, and enjoy on a deeply intrinsic level. They follow their favorite athlete in the media, or have hours-long discussions and debates about stats and the game or their beloved team. Super Bowl Sunday has become a weekend-long event, and at times it feels like a month-long event. Fans rally around athletes because they understand the hard work and determination it took them to condition themselves for the rigors of their sport. They realize that being a top athlete requires a great deal of diligence, patience, and endurance, and the ability to overcome adversity, and the fans appreciate that and can relate to it.

The world saw the awesome unifying power of sports at Wimbledon in 2002 when Aisam-Ul-Haq Qureshi, a Pakistani Muslim, and Amir Hadad, an Israeli Jew, overcame the differences that have divided their people for decades when they decided to play on the same side in the men's doubles draw. Given their nations' shared history, for them there could be so much more than loss of money, endorsements, or fans at stake. It was to me a very brave and powerful gesture, considering the history of their warring peoples.

Wimbledon is the oldest tennis tournament in the world and is considered by many to be the most prestigious. It is held at the All England Lawn Tennis and Croquet Club in Wimbledon, England, where the first game was played in 1877 on grass courts. For participants in the tournament, the physical and emotional training and buildup to playing some of the best players in the world is almost indescribable. Add to that the slippery grass courts, the huge crowds, and the mob of media, and it is clear that playing at Wimbledon under any circumstances is stressful. I could not imagine how Qureshi and Hadad felt the first day they stepped out onto the court to play on the same team, or what made them decide to play together. I knew there had been considerable fallout already for Qureshi. After the announcement of his doubles partner, Qureshi's country's sports board made headlines when it threatened to ban him if he played with Hadad. A July 2002 headline in the *Daily Telegraph* proclaimed: "Muslim Who Plays with Jew Faces Tennis Ban."

To fully understand how important a gesture it was for Qureshi and Hadad to take the same side in their doubles match, we have to understand the Palestinian-Israeli conflict. In an article written in *The Higher Learning* in June 2014, Mbiyimoh Ghogomu explains it this way:

It all started after World War II.

With millions of Jews displaced because of the Holocaust, the United Nations was looking for a good place to establish a Jewish state.

At the time Palestine was actually a British colony, and the UN figured that Palestine (which included Jerusalem, the center of the Jewish faith) was the best place to establish the new Jewish state of Israel.

So, in late November, 1947, the UN passed Resolution 181, which divided the Palestinian territory into Jewish and Arab states.

The Palestinian Arabs who were living there at the time refused to recognize the agreement. They had been told (by the United States) that no decisions would be made without consulting them. They also felt the agreement was too favorable to the Jews, at the expense of the local Palestinians.

So, as soon as the resolution was passed, fighting began, with Arab forces attacking Israeli territories that had formerly been part of Palestine before UN Resolution 181.

The fighting intensified when Israel declared independence a year later.[1]

According to *This Day in History*:

On May 14, 1948, in Tel Aviv, Jewish Agency Chairman David Ben-Gurion proclaims the State of Israel, establishing the first Jewish state in 2,000 years. In an afternoon ceremony at the Tel Aviv Art Museum, Ben-Gurion pronounced the words "We hereby proclaim the establishment of the Jewish state in Palestine, to be called Israel," prompting applause and tears from the crowd gathered at the museum. Ben-Gurion became Israel's first premier.

In the distance, the rumble of guns could be heard from fighting that broke out between Jews and Arabs immediately following the British army withdrawal earlier that day. Egypt launched an air assault against Israel that evening. Despite a blackout in Tel Aviv—and the expected Arab invasion—Jews joyously celebrated the birth of their new nation, especially after word was received that the United States had recognized the Jewish state. At midnight, the State of Israel officially came into being upon termination of the British mandate in Palestine.[2]

The conflict has continued since then, as Israel and Palestine both feel a claim to the land. Since 1946, Palestinian land has shrunk monumentally and hundreds of thousands of Palestinian Arabs have been displaced. The ensuing territorial dispute between the Palestinians and Israelis has had a long and tumultuous history, one that continues to this day. The separation of key cities within the country has decimated many of those areas, and security checkpoints and strict control of borders create divisions and discord.

Today, the Palestinian territory is split into two parts, each area controlled by a different faction. Gaza is governed by the militant Islamic organization Hamas, while the Palestinian areas of the West Bank are controlled by the secular Palestine Liberation Organization (PLO). While Gaza is entirely Palestinian, the West Bank is split into three zones, under different control: strictly Palestinian, joint Palestinian and Israeli, and strictly Israeli.

Ramallah is the de facto capital of the West Bank. To get there you have to cross a wall built by Israel that encircles the entire West Bank. Construction of the thick, high four-hundred-mile concrete wall began in 2002 with the purpose of putting a barrier between the territories. Though there is a coil of barbed wire above it, every year, one way or another, forty thousand Palestinians make it over the wall. Palestinian movement is monitored by Israeli checkpoints to control the flow of people. The first is the Qalandia Checkpoint. Palestinians hold different ID cards depending on whether they are from the West Bank, Gaza, or East Jerusalem, which dictates where and when they can travel in the region.

Checkpoints are inevitable on even short journeys, and curfews can be implemented at any time. There are arbitrary controls regardless of what your documents say as to whether or not you will be allowed past a given checkpoint. Theoretically the only people allowed to travel freely across the regions are foreigners, but access can still be denied at any time for any reason by Israeli checkpoint controls. When you cross the first checkpoint you arrive in Ramallah, West Bank, which is one of Palestine's most liberal cities. However, many women still cover up in traditional Islamic dress.

Shuhada Street was once the center of commerce and the hub of Palestinian tailoring until 1994, but the Israeli army closed down hundreds of businesses as Israeli settlers moved into the area. All trade stopped. Now the street is mostly deserted, and the shops are not only closed but their doors are welded shut. Today about five hundred Israeli settlers live there and are guarded by a patrol of Israeli soldiers.

Erez Crossing is the checkpoint at the border to the Israeli Gaza Strip. For all its notoriety, Gaza is a strip of land only twenty-five miles long and six miles wide infamous for its sustained periods of violent conflict. Gaza is governed by the militant Islamic group Hamas, which is listed as a foreign terrorist organization by the US government. Since Hamas took control of the Gaza Strip in 2007, both Israel and Egypt have held Gaza under a blockade, shutting down its borders and allowing Gazans to leave only under exceptional circumstances. In 2008 and 2014 full-scale wars broke out with Israel, the latter of which killed thousands of people, the majority of them Palestinian.

Entering Gaza is heavily restricted. Palestinians living in the West Bank are not allowed access to Gaza and vice versa. Crossing its borders is difficult because you must pass a series of heavy Israeli security checks, then walk through a two-mile-long fully enclosed caged tunnel, which is topped by barbed wire. This tunnel leads you to a final hurdle, the Hamas checkpoint. Despite a years-long conflict and war-torn towns, Gaza is quite beautiful. Its beach on the Mediterranean Sea shares the same waters as the South of France. The waters off Gaza after a certain point are controlled by the Israeli navy. There is a limited area Gazans are allowed out to sea of about three miles; beyond that they cannot cross without risking being shot.

There are daily power outages, with power on for several hours, then off for several hours. The Erez border is the way out of Gaza City back to the West Bank and Ramallah. Palestinians are not allowed into Jerusalem without a permit, but Americans can easily come and go with their passports. However, if you have an American passport *and* a Palestinian ID card there are restrictions. In that case, you can travel to Jerusalem only within certain times of the day and there is a curfew of 9:00 p.m. Americans can drive through the checkpoint; however, Palestinians must walk through the security gate into East Jerusalem. There is often tear gas and rubber bullets fired at the Palestinians at the checkpoint, during protests and demonstrations.

The Beit-El Checkpoint and the Qalandia Checkpoint take you back into East Jerusalem.

There is no easy way to fully explain the differences between Palestine and Ramallah in the West Bank, and Jerusalem and Gaza in the east, for the people living there under the conditions dictated by religion, and their shared history, and location. Their life is defined by borders more so than any other place I can think of.

It was with this shared history as a politically charged and divided people that Aisam-Ul-Haq Qureshi, a Pakistani

Muslim, and Amir Hadad, an Israeli Jew, made the decision to team up. Qureshi faced immediate pushback from his government and hate mail from Islamic radicals. His national tennis association threatened him with expulsion if he played on the same team with Hadad. Saulat Abbas, the director of the Pakistan Sports Board, issued an "official condemnation" of Qureshi for playing with an Israeli, adding, "An explanation has been sought from him. Since Pakistan has no links with Israel, Qureshi may face a ban."[3] In contrast, the Israeli Tennis Association gave Hadad its full support. In the face of the backlash against Qureshi, Hadad said, "Aisam and I are friends first, and Arabs or Jews second."

In spite of the threat of a ban, Qureshi stood firm. He knew he had a good chance of winning for his country if he played with Hadad, who was excellent on grass courts. Asked how he would respond to the ban, Qureshi replied, "That would be their own loss. If they [the federation] want to stay in the lower levels, that's fine. I'm going to stay and play for them, but if I believe I could do well with Amir in the big events, the Grand Slams, I'll stay and play with him. Why not?"[4]

When I spoke to Qureshi about his experiences and what made him and Hadad decide to play together, I was struck that neither he nor Hadad considered it a political statement. It made sense to them from a tennis perspective. They were simply a strong team together because of their unique talents. As we discussed the events leading up to the tournament it became clear that Qureshi was first and foremost playing for his nation, while also representing all tennis players in a show of unity and sportsmanship.

"Amir and I happened to be at the tournament office during the Wimbledon qualifying deadline," Qureshi told me while training in Doha. "Both of us had no partners, so we decided to sign in and give it a shot. I have known him for a while and knew he was good on grass courts and had a good sense of doubles—not once did it ever cross my mind that he was a Jew or from Israel. Amir is a great guy, and I got along well with him and other players from Israel. I did not know him that well off the court, but we would greet each other, as we did all the other players.

"Our doubles partnership raised a lot of questions back home in Pakistan, and my sports board and federation even announced that they would ban me from playing for my country if I continued to play at Wimbledon or at any other tournament with Hadad. But I stood my ground and kept playing with him, and the Association of Tennis Professionals (ATP) even gave us both an Arthur Ashe humanitarian award. After the match we stayed in touch for a while but then he retired. I still ask other Israeli players on the tour about him.

"Our doubles partnership made a huge impact in my life and surely in a positive way.

"In 2010 when I made the finals with Rohan Bopanna, who is a Hindu and an Indian, there were only praises from both sides, and my people and federation and sports board realized from my partnership with Amir in Wimbledon as well as with Rohan that all I was trying to do was to get acclaim for my country and my family. Playing with Amir and Rohan both helped me in achieving that, and I was honored with another Arthur Ashe award from the ATP.

"Would I do it again? I would surely do it again because I truly believe that we should not mix politics, religion, color, or race with sports. Sport teaches us to be equal and to judge and treat a person as a human being and not because of their race, their religion, or what country they come from."

Despite the backlash and just qualifying for Wimbledon, Hadad and Qureshi made it to the round of sixteen of the men's doubles and became fan favorites. Although they did not win the match, they won an even greater victory when they put their nations' decades of animosity aside, ignored the potential backlash, and presented a unified front on the tennis court. Hadad and Qureshi's decision was not only courageous, it was historic because it united their two nations for the first time in nearly sixty years, on the tennis court.

The Refugee Crisis Through the Lens of Sports

The recent escalation of the refugee crisis resulted in a controversial executive order on immigration, signed by US president Donald Trump in January 2017, that barred refugees and citizens from seven Muslim-majority countries—Iraq, Iran, Libya, Somalia, Sudan, Syria, and Yemen—from entering the United States. The backlash was immediate and fierce as images of handcuffed families and even children, detained for hours at airports, swept international news and social media. Protestors across the country and the world marched against the ban. Many state representatives across party lines called the ban unconstitutional. Federal courts in New York and California immediately blocked parts of the ban from being implemented. The US Ninth Circuit Court of Appeals ruled 3–0 to uphold a lower federal court's ruling that put the nationwide immigration ban on hold. It was argued that the ban sought to classify refugees as terrorists. According to Human Rights Watch, the number of Americans killed annually by jihadist immigrant extremists is two. The number of Americans killed by being shot by another American is 11,737.

America is a young country made up almost entirely of immigrants. The only natives to this country are Native Americans. So many of the people who made America the innovative country it is today are either immigrants or refugees, and this is particularly true in sports. Often athletes came to America seeking asylum from war, or fleeing famine, persecution, and restrictive policies. Many of these athletes then became American citizens and went on to represent the country in the Olympics and brought home medals. Among them are the tennis player Martina Navratilova from Czechoslovakia, and the Eritrean American distance runner Meb Keflezighi, whose family fled war, famine, and persecution in Eritrea, East Africa, and eventually settled in the United States.

Keflezighi was born during the deadly three-decade war for liberation from Ethiopia. Because his father, Russom, was a liberation supporter, he had to flee his family home in Adi Beyani to escape Ethiopian soldiers. Keflezighi's mother, Awetash, who feared that her husband would be killed, convinced him to leave Ethiopia. He ended up in Milan, Italy, for five years, sending money back to his family until he could afford to bring them to Italy in 1986. The family then immigrated to the United States in 1987.

Keflezighi started running in school and began winning distance races. In 2009 he won the New York City Marathon (and in 2014 the Boston Marathon, becoming the first American man to win both races since 1982 and 1983). He went on to become the 2004 Olympic marathon silver medalist. He finished fourth in the 2012 Summer Olympics. He came in fourth in the 2014 New York City Marathon, eighth in the 2015 Boston Marathon, and second in the 2016 US Olympic team trials to qualify for the 2016 Summer Olympics.

Keflezighi is an inspiration, and despite his tumultuous childhood, he has kept a positive outlook and filtered that positivity into activism and philanthropy. His MEB ("Maintaining Excellent Balance") Foundation supports programs that empower youth, their families, and their communities. It also funds programs that engage children in academics, and encourages health and fitness through sports.

Keflezighi was a refugee, along with the other members of his large family, and his take on the refugee situation now and when he first arrived in the 1980s is illuminating and insightful. I met with Keflezighi in San Diego to talk to him about his unique and amazing journey from Eritrea to the United States, and if that journey helped him to persevere as an athlete.

"My family came to the US because we wanted to get away from the war," Keflezighi said during our conversation. His accent is still apparent even after so many years in the United States. "Growing up in Eritrea during the war, you didn't know what tomorrow would bring, you didn't know what the future held for you. You had very few opportunities. I grew up in a village that didn't have electricity or running water. If I had stayed I would probably have been a farmer.

"The war was for independence, and my father was an independence supporter. We knew we had to escape or we could end up in prison or we could be killed. So there was not much choice. We decided to take a chance and go to Sudan, which was 225 miles away. The journey was across wilderness. There were hyenas and snakes. In Sudan, we were separated from our father for five years while he was in Italy. He sent us clothes and whatever he could afford. We didn't have much. We shared our shirts, our jeans, all of it. The clothes he sent didn't always fit, but luckily I had siblings, so what didn't fit me would fit one of my brothers. Sometimes it was difficult; it was like the makeshift soccer games we would play. We had the long socks, but no shoes. So we just played with whatever we found in ditches. It was hard, but I have good memories of playing soccer without shoes or even a plastic ball that bounced.

Eventually my father was able to send for us and we went to Italy. Then we came to the United States. It was a blessing for us to come to the United States. I'm telling you this just so you have appreciation for everything that you had as a child. Food to eat, to be able to play sports or you know, make pictures with your pencil. We didn't take any of this for granted."

Given that Keflezighi came here as a refugee, I wanted his perspective on both the 2017 executive order to limit refugees and today's political climate. Some Americans have argued that the refugee-vetting process is extreme enough, while others don't think it is. Some people argue that it's a matter of safety; others feel it might be about something else, whether that is discrimination, bias, or even xenophobia. I wanted to know his thoughts, given that Keflezighi and his family have been through that refugee program.

"Like my family, ninety to ninety-five percent of the people that come here, come with the best intentions," Keflezighi

answered. "Why not help them? I don't think the ban is fair
to women and their children. Five-year-olds, eight-year-olds. I
can understand if there are eighteen-year-olds or twenty-two-
year-olds. Sure, do more background checks, do a thorough
background check. But not when it is a wife, mother, or widow
coming with three children . . .

"We came here looking for refuge, to eat and feel safe from
war. We were willing to work. Nothing is guaranteed when
you come here. Nothing is handed to you. I was lucky to have
a god-given talent as a runner but I was willing to work at it.
It was never by accident that I got a good grade in a class. I
worked hard and was studious. It is the same for the refugees
coming to the States now. What we achieve here is not by accident, and we give back because this is now our country too.
We become runners, athletes, engineers, doctors, poets or writ-
ers or filmmakers. We contribute. As an athlete who achieved
some sort of success, I've made it my goal to help someone else
achieve success. I think some of the fear is that we are not as
social as in the past and I don't mean social media. We need
to be more interactive people. We are always on the Internet,
which makes us solitary and internal. We lose a feeling of community when we don't even know who our neighbors are."

I agree with Keflezighi's perspective. Today, more than
ever, our country feels divided and divisive. We are operating
more on fear and a need to isolate ourselves. But that is never
the answer. We should instead make an effort to get to know
our neighbors, especially if they are different, ethnically, cul-
turally, or religiously from us. So much of our communication
today isn't personal, it is digital, especially via social media such
as Twitter, Facebook, or Instagram. We don't have as much of

a personal interaction with one another anymore. That has its positive side, such as giving athletes the ability to easily reach their fans, but the downside is that less of our interaction is on a personal level. This doesn't allow us as citizens to really get to know our neighbors or our community. And if they are different from us, all we know is what we see in the media or read about, which could contribute to fear. That makes it so much easier to fall victim to divisive rhetoric. As a refugee seeking asylum and now as an American citizen, Keflezighi has experienced both aspects of exclusion and inclusion in American society. Does he think that there is a better way to approach the vetting system, a way that is more inclusive and less divisive yet still keeps the country safe?

"I can only speak from my own experiences when I first came here, but you have to think, as a country, how you are perceived when you are welcoming. When you make kind gestures, sweet gestures, they are never forgotten. I still remember the people who helped me when I first came here thirty years ago. We were in the welfare system. My father supplemented that by driving a taxi, and he helped out at restaurants. He did whatever he could. We came here to the US, and I started ninth grade. We didn't have much. A memory that has stayed with me is when the teachers at my school put together money to buy me a letterman jacket because my parents couldn't afford one. I remember things like that, acts of kindness. My foundation is my way of giving back for what was given to me. The opportunities I had by being in this country, to have the opportunity to run and to win races in New York and Boston, has put me in the position to use my voice and position to help others."

Keflezighi's background, what he experienced, the way he grew up, and the atrocities he saw in Eritrea made him want to make a better life here and also for others, and influenced him to start his foundation. Keflezighi wanted to give back for what he received here and for the kindness shown to him in this country. That is lost in today's discussion about refugees and immigrants. They are seeking asylum, but they give back tremendously to the country and in so many ways. The list of immigrants who have contributed to American culture and society is too long to list, but they are in every industry— sports, commerce, technology, media, manufacturing—and have changed the way America communicates or operates. We would not be the country we are today without their contributions. I think they make these contributions for a few reasons. One, they were welcomed here when they sought refuge, and two, they feel an affinity for and a sense of belonging to America after living here for so many years. And note that many immigrants become naturalized citizens. Considering the divisiveness the immigration ban is creating in our country and in the world I wanted to know if Keflezighi thought he would feel welcome in the US today, the way he was welcomed when he first arrived. His response was immediate and emphatic.

"I was welcome here in 1987. But now, no." Keflezighi shook his head. "There's been so many attacks that happened all over the country and world. Now people have to think twice before becoming a refugee or immigrating. In my experience and from my own perspective I think that's unfair, obviously, because when you're kind there's going to be kindness returned. There are so many people who are coming here to do positive things. When we come here and feel welcomed, a seed blossoms. You want to give back to repay that kindness, to show appreciation, to help the country that welcomed you and gave you refuge."

Keflezighi won the Boston Marathon the year after the bombing attack at the race killed three people and injured more than 260. I could only imagine that for him, winning was particularly special after the horrible tragedy there the year before. What was the crowd like and the feeling that year?

Keflezighi's eyes lit up as he answered. "I was the first person CNN interviewed who was an African American with an accent so it was very special. Especially after the bombing the year before. Many people, refugees, immigrants, visa holders, wanting to come here stopped going to that airport in Boston right after it happened. You feel singled out, like more eyes are on you. It's always unfortunate when something like that happens, but that it was caused by immigrants. The bombing. The year I won the Boston Marathon I wanted to do something positive. Whether it was winning, whether it was doing something for the families that it affected. That was my goal, to try to bring us all together."

Meb Keflezighi wanted to do something positive during the 2014 Boston Marathon. He wanted to bring people together after the tragic bombing the year before. And he did. When he crossed the finish line, as a former refugee who is now an American citizen, he showed the world that the divisive acts of a few do not represent the majority of refugees and immigrants who live in the United States and want to do good and be a positive influence here. As a former refugee and an immigrant, Keflezighi showed that we cannot and should not be divided by ethnicity, religion, race, or sex. It does more harm than good and engenders resentment and a lack of unity. He was so determined to replace the negative act of the year before with a positive one that he not only won the marathon, but did it in record time and set a personal best.

How Sports Changes Perceptions and Lives

The idea that sports changes lives and perceptions is more than a slogan on a T-shirt or a way to sell merchandise. Anyone who has become more assured or developed a competitive edge by mastering a sport, or felt the camaraderie of being a part of a team, understands how sports can make you more confident, more focused, more determined, and more driven. Playing a sport, training your mind and your body to excel, can change not only your perception of yourself but also how others perceive you.

We find evidence of this in the most unlikely of places: a refugee camp in the middle of the desert. It was there that a group of girls, living in one of the most traditional and conservative countries in the Middle East, came together as a team. These young women who had never played sports before changed not only their families' and community's perception of them, but also their perception of themselves and of what they could do and be. Displaced by the war in Syria and living in Za'atari refugee camp in Jordan, these sheltered young women excelled in a game that was forbidden, but ultimately helped to spread a message of female empowerment, hope, and inspiration. It also strengthened their community and their families, and allowed them to escape from the daily life as refugees in war-torn Syria.

Women's soccer has become one of the most exciting and popular sports, one in which standouts like Mia Hamm and Megan Rapinoe have electrified the field, without their gender downplaying their prowess and athleticism. Thousands of miles away in a harsh Middle Eastern desert a group of young girls also changed the perception of soccer and a girl's role in sports, yet none of them had kicked a soccer ball until a few months earlier. In the blinding, arid desert, two Syrian girls' teams played the biggest game of their lives. Soccer was a sport that until then they were not allowed to play because of their religion. That day, they changed perceptions of what girls are capable of and challenged traditional beliefs.

Sarah Leah Whitson, the Middle East executive director of Human Rights Watch, has called the war in Syria "one of the greatest humanitarian and political catastrophes we are facing." Bashar al-Assad, the president of Syria since 2000, has used Scud missiles, military planes, and other weapons to quash the uprising against what a large part of the population considers dictatorial rule.[5] According to BBC News:

> When protests against his government began in March 2011 he gave orders to crush the dissent, rather than tolerate it, and he refused to meet protesters' demands.
>
> The brutal crackdown by the security forces did not, however, stop the protests and eventually triggered an armed conflict that the UN says has so far left more than 250,000 people dead.

More than 11 million others have been forced from
their homes as forces loyal to Mr Assad and those opposed to his rule battle each other—as well as jihadist
militants from Islamic State (IS).[6]

The brutal ongoing war in Syria has displaced and separated families, moved them from their homes to refugee camps
miles away in the middle of the desert, and left them shell-
shocked from the daily onslaught of gunfire and mortar fire.
It was one of those mortar shells that killed twenty-nine students and a teacher when it slammed into their school outside
Damascus. The death tolls rose on a daily basis as dead bodies
pummeled by rocket fire piled up in the streets, and the cloy-
ing odor of burning cars filled the air. These are the memories
that thirteen-year-old Rama Khalid Jwaba and her six sisters
and brother took with them when they left Syria and headed
west to Jordan, to a refugee camp eight miles from the Syrian
border.

"It was a miserable experience. It was terrifying. You could
expect to be bombed or have a rocket fired at you," Rama's
sister Roweda recalled. Rama and her family were driven from
their home in Daraa, a city in the southwest corner of Syria.
Daraa was the catalyst for the Syrian civil war in 2011 when
a dozen teenagers were arrested and tortured for painting
antigovernment graffiti. Rather than hear out the protesters'
demands for a more democratic government in Syria, Assad
instead responded by commanding his soldiers to fire into a
crowd of protestors. They then went house to house and arrested people they thought were involved in the protest, cap-
turing and torturing thousands of people.

Afraid that the army would arrest her brother, Rama's family joined the millions fleeing Syria and headed west to Jordan in January 2013 as violence escalated. On the day they left, a neighborhood village was being bombed by jets. They had made it out in just the nick of time. Rama remembers being terrified. After an exhausting journey across the desert, they arrived in Za'atari, a massive makeshift refugee camp in Jordan less than eight miles from the Syrian border. Three years ago, the spot on which the camp sits was just a desert in Jordan. Today, it is home to 82,000 residents and is Jordan's fourth-largest city.

Life in Za'atari is hard. Jobs are scarce and resources are few. Electricity is unreliable, shutting off for hours at a time. Food and water are strictly rationed, and the camp eventually had to close its gates and not allow any more refugees because of limited resources. Rama's only brother has returned to Syria to look for work to help the family. Rama goes to school for three hours in the morning. The remainder of her time is spent keeping the house, cooking and cleaning, and going to the mosque. In her spare time she wonders if her brother is okay and if he will return. As with most women in conservative Muslim families, Rama's traditional role is in the home. Traditional girls in Za'atari start getting married when they are sixteen. Their childhood is cut short alternately by war, displacement, and marriage. The general belief is that girls should stay home and not go outside.

But that did not stop Prince Ali bin al-Hussein, the third son of King Hussein, the king of Jordan, from starting an unprecedented sports program that introduced many girls to a forbidden sport. Prince Hussein is FIFA's top lieutenant. The

Fédération Internationale de Football Association (FIFA) is an association governed by Swiss law founded in 1904 and based in Zurich. It has 211 member associations, with delegates from Belgium, Denmark, France, the Netherlands, Spain, Sweden, and Switzerland. Its goal is the constant improvement of football. In America we call it soccer.

As FIFA notes, "the founders [of the organization] created the first FIFA statutes, unifying the laws of the game to make it fair and clear to all players setting the foundation for all future soccer development. . . . Football has the power to bring people together and to break down barriers. It gives FIFA a platform to improve standards of education, health and sustainability, and to raise living standards and quality of life across the world."[7]

FIFA's website goes on to describe the history of organized soccer as follows: "Known as the world's favorite game, football began in 1863 in England, when rugby football and association football branched off on their different courses and the Football Association in England was formed, becoming the sport's first governing body. The rules and the structure of soccer provide a common, simple language to support unity through fair play and peaceful interactions."[8]

In one of the most conservative countries in the world, many believe that sports are not for women and that girls should not play sports at all, especially not soccer. Their doing so went against traditional beliefs. That was one of the challenges Prince Hussein faced. The second was to try to have them play but within the rules of the community. Girls cannot play in front of people, and definitely not in front of males. To abide by those rules, the soccer team enclosed one of the boys' sports fields, trained all female coaches, and then recruited girls. One day, Rama was sitting outside her house watching the girls play. The coach saw her and invited her into the game. The first time Rama asked her father if she could play, he said no. The second time she asked him, he said no, but she went anyway.

The sports program, which started with very little interest and only a few girls, has since grown to forty coaches and over four hundred participants. Since the girls have been playing, it is clear that it has changed them. They are happier and more relaxed. They laugh more and cry less. They thrive under the camaraderie of their teammates and the competition of the sport. Although having played for only three months, Rama has excelled at soccer and is one of her team's best players. When the boys see Rama practicing in front of her house, their mouths drop open in amazement because they thought girls could not play soccer—and certainly not the way Rama plays.

Rama's team did remarkably well and qualified for the summer tournament, and although they would play without an audience, they didn't seem to mind. They were happy to be together, playing as a team, proudly wearing their blue team shirts. The girls shouted, skipped, threw their hands in the air, and clapped when their teammates scored, the memories of their war-torn homeland and its horrors momentarily forgotten. The difference from the shy girls they were a few months earlier to the confident, athletic young women playing that day was astounding.

After four wins, Rama's team easily beat its next competitor. They would play the championship game the next morning. This time they would play in front of the community, and their friends and family. Rama's family had never seen her or her team play soccer in a game. On the morning of the final, Rama and her teammates were incredibly nervous. As she walked with her family to the field, her father said, "Don't be nervous. It's only a game. Just do your best." But Rama was worried that she would lose. "No you won't," he told her. "Just stay focused." His reluctance for her playing was forgotten and in its place there was a pride that his daughter was the best player on the team.

When they arrived at the field, friends and family packed the sidelines. The girls from the other soccer programs were there, to cheer them on. And the boys were also there, excited to see their first girls' soccer game. The support from the community was overwhelming. As the teams lined up and prepared to start the game, you could see the nervousness on Rama's and her teammates' faces. They were anxious to be playing in front of such a large crowd. As the teams took their places on a makeshift soccer field in the middle of the desert, under the bright sun, a hush settled over the crowd. This was for them a moment like no other. Girls were playing other girls in soccer, and the whole community was there to cheer them on.

At first, the girls were clearly nervous. But they soon forgot the screaming crowd and focused on the game and became lost in it. Rama's team played well. Fighting for the ball, the opposite team took the lead and fought to keep it. Rama's team lost 1–0, and it was heartbreaking. The girls cried and tried to comfort each other. But in the end they knew that day ultimately was not about winning. Rama and the other girls proved to their community: girls can play sports, and they can play well.

Rama's father struggled to describe his feelings on that day as he watched his daughter on the field. "I was surprised. I never thought she was that good. I had a feeling I can't describe. I can't really express it." That day Rama and her teammates earned the right to call themselves soccer players. Although still surrounded by the upheaval of war, the lessons learned on the soccer field, from the coaches and teammates, have left an indelible mark on Rama and her teammates, and on all the girls on the teams. Their experiences have changed them, transformed perceptions, and inspired them and others. But mostly it has shown them that they can do and be anything, even athletes. It has shown them not only the power of sports, but also their own power and resilience, and gave them hope in an unlikely place. That day, those girls on the field quietly created change by changing perceptions of what girls are capable of.

Creating Change, Quietly

Martina Navratilova is the epitome of a natural activist. She stood up for what she believed in at a huge personal risk. She was and still is outspoken, and was an activist simply by being herself, at a time when most professional athletes were still closeted. Navratilova didn't know if she would see her family again when she defected from Czechoslovakia. When she became a naturalized US citizen, she felt that she was finally free to speak out. She knew she could lose sponsorships or fans, or that public opinion might turn against her, but she didn't have to fear for her life or her family's life the way she might have back in Czechoslovakia. She has never shied away from any issue. She freely spoke about what was on her mind in interviews, and when the questions started veering away from strictly tennis to topics with wide-ranging effects on society, she spoke out about those with her usual honesty and straightforwardness.

Born in Czechoslovakia in 1956, Martina Navratilova began playing tennis at a young age, and was one of the most dominant female tennis players in the world in the late seventies and early eighties. Later in life, she became active in the gay rights movement. Tennis was a part of Navratilova's DNA. Her grandmother Agnes Semenska had been an international player who had upset the mother of Vera Sukova, a 1962 Wimbledon finalist, in a national tournament.

Navratilova started at a very young age, then very quickly refined her game and rose up through the ranks. At four she was hitting tennis balls off of a cement wall. By age seven, Navratilova was playing regularly, spending hours on a court each day, working on her strokes and footwork. Navratilova began taking lessons at nine from the Czech champion George Parma, and she blossomed under his coaching. At age fifteen, she won the Czech national championship. In 1973, at sixteen, she turned pro and began competing in the United States. Navratilova defected to the United States when Czechoslovakia was under Communist control when she was eighteen. Leaving Czechoslovakia cut her off from her family, but it was also the start of her phenomenal tennis career. In 1978 she beat Chris Evert and won her first Grand Slam tournament at Wimbledon. Her second Wimbledon win came a year later with another victory over Evert. Navratilova's third Grand Slam title came at the Australian Open in 1981. By the early eighties she was the most dominant women's player in tennis.

During Navratilova's on-court success she was open about her sexual orientation. "I never thought there was anything strange about being gay," she wrote in her 1985 autobiography, *Martina.* Along the way, her public perception "advanced from animosity to acceptance to adulation." Her left-handed playing style, intimidating physicality, and power on the court set her aside from all the other female athletes. Navratilova was a poster girl for tomboys and girls who were not girly-girls but who were powerful and athletic and were proud of it.

Navratilova was one of the first tennis players who went against the mainstream perception of what female players should look like, or how they should play. Chris Evert, the darling of the tennis world at that time, was ultrafeminine and lithe. Meanwhile, Navratilova, European, almost 5'8", and at her heaviest 167 pounds, once caused tennis authority Bud Collins to describe her as "the Great Wide Hope." Almost polar opposites, Evert and Navratilova were often pitted against each other professionally and physically. But despite the media backlash and negative attention, Navratilova simply played her best and silenced her critics on the court.

Robert Lipsyte and Peter Levine wrote in *Idols of the Game*, "As a lesbian, Navratilova expanded the dialogue on issues of gender and sexuality in sports. In the years that she and Chris Evert were locked in their fierce rivalry to be Number One, sports fans saw it was possible for two very different women, physically and emotionally, different in lifestyle and playing style, to both be great champions—and friends."

Though she learned tennis playing on the slow clay courts of Czechoslovakia, Navratilova was not interested in the slow-moving, baseline-anchored woman's game of the time.

Instead, her game was one of a ferocious serve, powerful volley, then lightning speed as she rushed the net. Her emotional outbursts were stunning and may have been the precursor to Serena Williams's. Navratilova won three major singles titles before she was twenty-five, an age when many women players are ready to retire. She finished with eighteen titles, including four US Opens, three French, and two Australian. Adding in her thirty-eight doubles titles, Navratilova won fifty-six Grand Slam championships. Only the Australian Margaret Court has won more majors. And she is seventy-four.

Navratilova's influence, however, went far beyond the court.

In July 1981, soon after being granted US citizenship, she took the bold step of telling the truth when asked about her sexual preferences and said she was bisexual. Navratilova was also vocal about her affair with the author Rita Mae Brown.

"Martina was the first legitimate superstar who literally came out while she was a superstar," said Donna Lopiano, the executive director of the Women's Sports Foundation. "She exploded the barrier by putting it on the table. She basically said, this part of my life doesn't have anything to do with me as a tennis player. Judge me for who I am."

Although Navratilova's honesty cost her millions in endorsement opportunities because of corporate homophobia, she never backtracked or tried to fade into the background. On the contrary, even today, Navratilova speaks out for what she believes in. When US Supreme Court justice Ruth Bader Ginsburg called Colin Kaepernick's national anthem protest "dumb and disrespectful" in an interview with Katie Couric for Yahoo News, Navratilova spoke out against Ginsburg's comment. The *New York Times* reported that "while [Navratilova] also thinks Kaepernick's decision to kneel during the national anthem to protest police brutality and racial inequality 'may be somewhat disrespectful,'" she believed that athletes like him should be praised for speaking out on social issues—not shamed for it—especially when they do so in a peaceful way, as Kaepernick did. "So many athletes are afraid to use their platform to do the right thing and speak what they feel, and that's very depressing. . . . Sure, they are afraid of insulting people and losing money because of it, and everyone wants to make the maximum amount of money in their lifetime. But at the expense of who you are? I don't know. That just wasn't in my DNA."[9] A few days later, Ginsburg issued a statement apologizing for her comment. "I should have held my tongue," the statement read. "Barely aware of the incident or its purpose, my comments were inappropriately dismissive and harsh. I should have declined to respond."

Navratilova was never afraid to speak openly about what she felt needed to be changed in society. She publicly criticized George W. Bush for his conservative policies when he was president. She was also vocally critical of Bill Clinton for his "don't ask, don't tell" policy on gays in the military, which she felt neither addressed nor solved the issue. Navratilova also advocated for children's rights, animal rights, and gay rights and marriage equality.

Navratilova continues to speak up for human rights. In October 2016 at an event at the US State Department to discuss how to improve human rights at large international sports events, Navratilova called on entities like the International Olympic Committee and FIFA to ensure that their events are safe and open to everyone, without discrimination, and said doing so was a responsibility such organizations couldn't continue to shirk.

The More Things Change,
the More They Stay the Same

Martina Navratilova has never shied away from any issue. She spoke openly about what was on her mind in interviews. I was excited to speak with Navratilova about sports activism for many reasons. During such a highly political time in America, a time filled with so many polarizing issues, Navratilova's perspective—as both an immigrant who is now an American citizen, and also a longtime advocate and activist—would be enlightening, to say the least.

Navratilova made time to speak with me when she returned from vacation, right after the immigration ban was making headlines. I was not surprised that she had as much to say about the ban as about the importance of athletes speaking out about social justice. I wanted to begin by finding out what started Navratilova on the road to activism and if she ever felt that perhaps she had been too outspoken.

As usual she began with her trademark directness. "I became an activist just by being out, but I didn't actively look for it; it was by virtue of being who I was, where I was from. When I came here to the US as a political asylum seeker, it was an act of activism already. Being outspoken didn't happen until the nineties, when I really got behind the LGBT movement and became more involved in it. But I've been speaking out on various issues for as long as I can remember, whether it's the environment, animal rights, or kids. I had a children's foundation, Martina's Kids Foundation, back in the early eighties in Texas and I've always been outspoken.

"I remember getting into hot water speaking out about Magic Johnson. It's terrible that Magic has HIV. He's like a hero. I've met him and thought he was an amazing guy but what I said publicly at the time was, if a female athlete had contracted AIDS by sleeping with hundreds of men she'd be labeled a whore rather than a hero. I got such crap for that. And this is pre-Twitter. I would have had to get off Twitter if it existed back then. But that's how I was. I never skirted anything. It's not that I was so much of an activist as that I answered questions or even brought up subjects in press conferences, about tennis or whatever I was going through at the time. Journalists would then ask me more questions outside of the tennis realm or the sports realm. So I just always spoke what I thought, and I guess that in itself was an act of activism because so often during press conferences athletes don't talk about things outside of the game they just played."

When Navratilova commented on Magic Johnson, she was using her platform to call out a double standard that people in the public eye don't often do. She was pointing out that half of the population would have been treated differently had they been in the same position or circumstance— had it been a woman and not a man. In being as outspoken as Navratilova was, would she have had the same kind of ideas without her platform as a professional athlete? Her answer didn't surprise me.

"Yes. I would have found a way on a different level, but I would still be doing the same thing, or maybe something else, but I would be actively involved in something as I have been. I spoke out about issues, but I have also done a lot of charitable work. Because of the platform we professional athletes have we can do more good, we can reach more people. I'll play tennis for charity and make $50,000 for an hour of my work, so it's almost cheating. I was just reading about these women who ran from New York to Washington in protest in January. They hoped to raise $5,000 and they raised $100,000. But they ran two hundred or something miles, which is phenomenal. So we athletes with our kind of platform are kind of cheating."

Navratilova was referring to Alison Mariella Désir and Talisa Hayes, two women runners from Harlem. They ran the 240 miles from New York City to Washington, DC, right before the 2017 presidential inauguration to raise funds for Planned Parenthood. I was curious as to why Navratilova felt that being able to do good by doing something she loves like playing tennis felt a little like cheating. This was not a perspective I'd encountered during my talks with activist athletes.

"In a way, yes, it is a little like cheating," she answered. "Because it is so easy for us to reach our audience. As athletes I feel that yes, we do more, and get involved more than just the everyday Joe Blow or celebrities, actors, actresses, and other high-income, high-profile people. I think athletes do more than their fair share as far as giving their time and raising money for charity. For instance, James, you interact so closely with your fans and see a greater cross section of society as an athlete than a movie star. Actors make a movie then see their fans only during a premiere, or at an event, as opposed to the constant and instant interaction with fans that athletes have when they play tournaments and matches. Also sports, particularly tennis and golf, are so democratic. Those sports are just about how good you are and have nothing to do with anything else. It's purely based on your merit, and maybe because of that we feel that it is fair and we want to be fair-minded people."

Because I retired from professional tennis in 2013, before my incident with the NYPD, I am in many ways lucky. Any advocacy or activism I do now does not affect my play during a professional tour. Did Navratilova's activism or her speaking out or even being out ever affect her play, particularly while she was at the top of her game?

"Being out made me free. It freed me up," Navratilova answered, then paused, as though thinking back all those years to when she first immigrated to the United States. "When I left my country, that was the biggest pressure cooker ever, being out. Leaving Czechoslovakia and my family, not knowing if I would ever go back and see them, was pressure because when I left it was a one-way ticket. After that, everything was kind of a piece of cake. Being gay was not anything I was ever worried about. When I realized I was gay, it was literally like, oh that's what that was. I thought my life will never be as easy as I wanted it to be, but that's what it is and that was literally the amount of thought I gave it.

"I never felt I had to justify myself and I never felt ashamed or anything, but it was a freeing thing to not have to *not* talk about it. Or have to say, 'I don't want to talk about it.' I had never really said that about anything, whether it was politics or causes. I had always spoken out. So not to speak out about who I am was hard. And I didn't say anything because I was covering for other people who I was with who were in the closet. Initially I couldn't come out because I might not get my citizenship; that could have disqualified me back then. But the irony was I left my country so I could be free, but I wasn't really free until I was completely out. Now I don't have to hide anything at all, so it was really freeing.

"I think it made me a better tennis player because I didn't have any extra energy going anywhere except to my tennis. But at the same time it did make people cheer against me after I came out. There was no doubt about that. Now I would have a bigger fan base or it would be a wash. Then, maybe five percent of people approved of homosexuality. Everybody else was very negative. It did affect me when I was playing, especially when I was winning. I was never the home team. I get jealous to this day of Nadal and Federer, you know, Jesus, the crowd is always cheering for them. [Laughs.] They're the home team everywhere they go. I never had that until the very end of my career. But by then I wasn't winning as much anymore and people were more accepting of gays. So, it was a plus on one side but a minus because I really wanted to have that support or fifty-fifty.

"Looking back now, I don't think I realized what a positive effect it had on me to be out. Not that I ever really hid it, but I didn't have to even think about it anymore or watch what I said or didn't say. It was really since 1984 that it became much easier for me all the way around."

If anyone has advice on advocacy and speaking out for what you believe in, it would be this longtime activist and outspoken champion. Did Navratilova have any advice for athletes today who have something they are passionate about, who have a cause that is dear to them, or who feel the need to speak out about social justice or inequality? Also, did she think today's activist culture is different than it was in the seventies and eighties, when she was playing professionally?

"It's almost a selfish thing because it makes you feel good to help people," Navratilova responded in her usual straight-forward way. "You can affect people in a positive way and it takes so little of your time or effort to speak up for them. It helps them not feel so alone. Whether it's people of color, or of certain religions, or sexuality, whatever. Just to know that someone who is important, who has done well, has your back is extremely empowering for people. We athletes have such an opportunity to do that, especially now when you can connect so much easier with your fans with Twitter and social media. But I still get disappointed in some athletes who have a chance to speak out but don't because they don't want to upset some-body who might buy their sneakers or rackets. Let's put it all in perspective about what's really important. Is it for you to have another deal or make more money or to actually uplift thousands of people by what you do and what you say?

"It seems to me like the more things change the more they stay the same." She sighed deeply, as though she had seen what we're going through today as a country, all before. "We're still dealing with the same sexism, racism, phobias, or isms that we were then," she continued. "Now they're coming out more be-cause of the current political climate. My eleven-year-old goes to private school. She came home the other day and told me that a boy in school said that if I'm not careful Trump will deport me. She replied to him, But aren't you from Mexico? I think you're going back to Mexico first. So she went right back at him, but seriously, kids think this is okay. Eleven-year-old kids, and by the way, his family voted for Hillary Clinton, but it's in his head that it's okay to say things like that because he's hearing it.

"It's pretty scary nowadays. All these phobias are coming out, so it's even more important to speak out now because we seem to be going backwards. The possibilities are endless today with social media. You can definitely be heard and connect with your fans and make a difference in a much faster and easier way. At the same time you subject yourself to a lot of negativity, so it takes a strong person to speak out still. Especially with the immigration ban. As if they haven't suffered enough and they've already been vetted for two years.

"'Extreme vetting,' what does that even mean? It's all so subliminal and nonspecific that you can't really attack it, and it's done on purpose that way. But to make these blanket statements and have blanket bans, blanket anything is just horrible. To put everybody in the same basket seems self-defeating. To me, everything should be done on a case-by-case basis. That executive order was just horrible. People are either the best or the worst today, there is no in between. [Mike] Pence is terrible but he won't blow up the world. With him it will be the fight for human rights and gay rights all over again, but at least, he won't blow up the world."

Serbia: The Swimming Pool Alumni

We have to wonder why historically, professional athletes, almost more than any other group, have been the catalysts for social change. To answer that question we should look at the journey athletes often take to excel in their sport, and to train their mind and body to persevere. For athletes to be the best they can be in their sport, they must often overcome not only their competition but also their self-doubt, their backgrounds, or their own physical or financial circumstances. The sports world is built on inspirational stories of phenomenal achievements of athletes prevailing over unimaginable obstacles. It is often these very trials and tribulations that not only make them the fierce competitors they are but also inform their worldview, and inspire—no, compel—them to reach back to help others in the same situations.

In war-torn Serbia, two aspiring young tennis players fought against all odds to find a place where they could practice in safety from early-morning air raids. That place happened to be an empty swimming pool in an often bombed city. Novak Djokovic and Ana Ivanovic grew up amidst the hum of low-flying bombs during the Balkan conflict. The swimming pool in which they practiced had been drained and outfitted with makeshift tennis nets and green carpeting. That they both rose to be number one in their tennis careers is a testament to their strength of will and is inspirational not only to promising athletes and anyone facing seemingly overwhelming obstacles, but also to all the people of their homeland.

Serbia is a country known for war crimes perpetrated at the hands of Slobodan Milosevic, its former president. Under his rule, the Serbian people faced atrocities including genocide and crimes against humanity in connection with wars in Bosnia, Croatia, and Kosovo.

Imagine being twelve years old in the midst of the bloody conflict ravaging your city. Imagine the drone of low-flying bombers during daily air raids, the horrors of brutal ethnic cleansing, food and water shortages, and buildings and windows shaking from bombs dropped nearby. These things were part of Ivanovic's childhood, yet she was no different from any child. She grew up with her younger brother Milos, whom she liked to play basketball with. Her mother, Dragana, a lawyer, and her father, Miroslava, a self-employed businessman, tried to shield their children from the horrors outside their door.

Ivanovic developed a passion for tennis at five years old after watching her fellow Yugoslav Monica Seles on television. She begged her parents to buy her a racket and then memorized the telephone number of a local tennis clinic from an advertisement. With the local tennis courts destroyed or too expensive for the family to afford, Ivanovic spent freezing winters practicing her strokes in an abandoned Olympic-size swimming pool not far from her home. The aspiring tennis player rose before the sun to practice at six o'clock during lulls in the regular morning raids. Ivanovic, along with her fellow teen players Jelena Jankovic and Novak Djokovic, had ninety-minute practices in the makeshift tennis court and often played against each other. They would sometimes have to hide in a bomb shelter during surprise air raids.

Finding tennis facilities to practice in was only the start of her difficulties. Her parents were living on just a few hundred euros a month, barely able to meet the costs of lessons, equipment, or travel to games. During the conflict, flights in and out of Belgrade were suspended. Ivanovic had to travel seven hours by bus to neighboring Hungary because it was impossible to get a visa out of Serbia for international tournaments.

Ivanovic's future was transformed by a fateful meeting with Dan Holzmann, a Swiss businessman with a passion for tennis. Holzmann was taking tennis lessons when his Serbian coach mentioned a girl in Belgrade who had an exceptional talent but no financial resources to improve. That girl was Ana Ivanovic, who at fourteen was the twenty-second-ranked junior player in the world, despite how difficult it was for her to get to tournaments, and her lack of money for good equipment, suitable training facilities, or professional coaches. Intrigued, Holzmann wanted to meet Ivanovic, and in 2002 Ana and her mother flew to Switzerland after he helped them secure visas.

When Holzmann asked Ivanovic what she wanted from life, she answered, "I want to be number one in the world." He decided then and there to offer her financial assistance. Holzmann would make monthly payments to her family. The money would be an interest-free loan, not a donation. The loan, which eventually reached around $305,000, enabled Ivanovic to hire a good coach and allowed her to play in mainstream junior tournaments.

Ivanovic left Serbia to train in Basel, Switzerland, because of better training facilities and coaching. Holzmann, who was now her manager, was also from Basel. Ivanovic and her mother stayed with him until they could afford an apartment. Holzmann flew to her next junior tournament in Rome, which she lost in the first round. Devastated, Ivanovic started to cry as she left the court. Afraid that Holzmann would abandon her because of her loss, she locked herself in the locker room for four hours. After Ivanovic was finally convinced that he believed in her, she improved. The same fighting spirit that got her through the freezing 6:00 a.m. practices in the converted pool while planes dropped bombs overhead gave her the drive she needed to focus on and improve her game.

Driven to succeed, Ivanovic reached the final of the 2004 Junior Wimbledon tournament at seventeen. That year she also held her own and came close to beating Serena Williams. The next year she won her first career singles title. By the end of 2006, Ivanovic was ranked fourteenth in the world, then the next year she climbed up to number four. She started 2008 strong, by reaching the final of the Australian Open. Her biggest victory to date came at the 2008 French Open, where she won her first Grand Slam singles title.

Ivanovic has to date won fifteen WTA Tour singles titles, and five International Tennis Federation (ITF) women's circuit singles titles. Ivanovic was the first Serbian woman to reach a Grand Slam final at Roland Garros since Monica Seles became at sixteen the youngest person to win the tournament in 1991. Eventually winning over $15 million in prize money, she was able to repay every penny to Holzmann, whose belief in her gave her the opportunity to reach her full potential.

Ivanovic's journey has been a testament to persevering and overcoming emotional obstacles not only for yourself but also for those who believe in you. She was lucky to have had early support, and she in turn gives back. As a UNICEF national ambassador for Serbia and ambassador of the Quercus Foundation, which helps children in underprivileged areas of the world, Ivanovic is a staunch advocate for children's rights, education, and health. In 2016 Ivanovic was honored by the Quercus Foundation as its female icon for International Women's Day. In accepting this honor and for her work as a Quercus ambassador, Ivanovic said, "The Serbian mentality is very determined; we are aware that you have to work hard to achieve something. That's the mind-set that has shaped me as a player more than anything else. I never gave up and was lucky enough to have met people who helped me. I worked hard and kept pushing myself."

Novak Djokovic was Ivanovic's practice partner in the pool. Born in 1987 in Belgrade, Djokovic is the eldest of three sons whose younger brothers are Marko and Djordje. His friends and family call him "Nole." Djokovic became interested in playing tennis at age four and went on to become the first Serbian player to be ranked number one by the ATP and the first male player representing Serbia to win a Grand Slam singles title. He became the number one tennis player in the world in 2011 and as of 2017 was ranked number two in men's singles tennis. He has also won three Australian Open titles, a US Open title, and he won Wimbledon at twenty-four. After Djokovic won Wimbledon in 2011, a hundred thousand people gathered to celebrate in front of Belgrade's Parliament.

Djokovic wasn't driven to tennis the way Ivanovic was, but they share a Monica Seles connection. It was a fluke that Djokovic started playing tennis. His family was athletic. His father, Srdjan, and his mother, Dijana, were skiing instructors, and Srdjan had been a competitive downhill skier. But no one in the family was a tennis player. Although Serbia has produced its share of talented players, such as Janko Tipsarevic, Nenad Zimonjic, Viktor Troicki, Ana Ivanovic, Jelena Jankovic, and Djokovic among them, as a nation, Serbia was traditionally more noted in team sports, like basketball, water polo, and volleyball, in which many Serbian teams have won Olympic medals and world and European championships. Serbian athletes have often trained in more-than-poor conditions, and they have frequently lacked the necessary financial resources, but despite everything, many of them have become worldwide champions.

Novak started playing on the tennis courts in Kopaonik, a resort town where his family lived and owned a restaurant, where he sometimes would work as a waiter. Kopaonik is a popular tourist and skiing area between Serbia and Kosovo. Improbably, that was where the Serbian government decided to build a tennis facility, and that was where Jelena Gencic, Djokovic's first trainer and coach, who had once coached Monica Seles, first noticed him. After working with Djokovic, Gencic proclaimed him as the biggest talent she had seen since Monica Seles.

"When Djokovic was six, he told his parents that it was his mission to become the No. 1 tennis player in the world," wrote a profile of the athlete in *The New Yorker*. "When he was eleven, NATO began bombing Belgrade. Each night at eight o'clock, as the air-raid siren sounded, the family would run to an aunt's apartment building, which had a bomb shelter. For seventy-eight nights, they crouched in darkness, praying amid the screams of F-117s. Djokovic kept up his tennis throughout the bombardment, playing on cracked courts bereft of nets. He writes, in *Serve to Win* . . . 'We'd go to the site of the most recent attacks, figuring that if they bombed one place yesterday, they probably wouldn't bomb it today.'"[10]

For almost three months Djokovic and his family and the rest of Belgrade lived in fear for their lives, uncertain what the next day would bring. "On 22 May 1999, I was celebrating my 12th birthday," Djokovic told the UK *Spectator* in 2013. "I don't like to remember this, but it is one of my strongest memories. That birthday celebration in the Serbian tennis club

Partisan, when everyone was singing 'Happy Birthday' while the aeroplanes were flying over the sky dropping bombs on Belgrade. I think that at that time I was too young to conceptualise what was happening. Instead, I learned to refocus and to not listen to the sirens. I learned to focus on pleasure in having so much 'free time' to play tennis. I thought if I focus on the talent I believed I had, I can be the No. 1, I can win Wimbledon one day. That determination was crucial in my development as a professional athlete. Even today I draw on those foundations."[11]

This early adversity taught Djokovic how to manage and overcome fear at a young age, and ultimately these experiences would help him persevere as a tennis player who could focus during stressful, high-stakes matches. During the war, the economy collapsed and his family struggled to survive. The country was under embargo, and families faced extreme poverty and hardship. Under those conditions, life is a struggle just to survive, and the development of children in any sport, let alone in tennis, seemed impossible. Knowing they had a talent with Novak, his father, Srdjan, sold the family's gold and borrowed money from a loan shark. They sent Novak to a tennis academy in Munich, while the family stayed in Serbia. Novak left his family at the age of twelve, with the weight of their expectations on his young shoulders. This was one of the two turning points in his life. He had to grow up overnight and adjust to living on his own, not depending on his parents.

Djokovic considers leaving home one of the major markers in his life, which would define him as an athlete and a man. He trained hard and entered the top 100 in 2005, at the age of eighteen. In 2007, he became the third-ranked player in the world. In 2008, he won the Australian Open, his first Grand Slam. Despite the hardship of his early life, Djokovic has a goofy sense of humor. His other nickname is "the Djoker." His spot-on imitations of other tennis players like Rafael Nadal and Roger Federer have endeared him to the crowds.

Djokovic's troubled childhood and the tough times his country faced deeply informed his worldview. He is the most famous person in Serbia; he is also the world's most famous Serbian. Never forgetting his roots or the struggles of the people in Serbia, Djokovic gives back through the Novak Djokovic Foundation, which he founded in 2001. The foundation gives grants to educational initiatives and encourages childhood sports and education in Serbia. Understanding the struggles of growing up in the midst of a war, Djokovic has geared his foundation to helping children from disadvantaged communities or areas of conflict to grow up, play, and develop in stimulating, creative, and safe settings. The foundation's motto is "Believe in Their Dreams," because although Djokovic is from a country that was in conflict, he was able to achieve his dream of becoming the number one tennis player in the world, with the help of his family, who believed in him and supported him. But first he had to not only dare to dream but also believe he could achieve it.

In Serbia, and in many other countries afflicted with famine, war, or poverty, Djokovic believes that children don't dare to dream big. They lack the access or means to an education, they are plagued by illness, or they have suffered the loss of their parents. He saw a lot of this in his home country, and he decided to focus most of his efforts on helping children in Serbia. He believes that through education, children can be part of the collective effort to decrease poverty and social exclusion. They can learn by his example that if you work hard and believe in yourself, anything is possible. Now that he is in a position to give back and create a legacy, Djokovic wants to focus on helping young people fulfill their dreams.

In 2015, Djokovic was appointed a UNICEF goodwill ambassador. His foundation partnered with the World Bank in August 2015 to promote early childhood education in Serbia. Following his historic 2016 Australian Open victory, in which he became the first player in the Open era to win the tournament six times, Djokovic donated $20,000 to Melbourne City Mission's early childhood education program to help disadvantaged children.

And as a UNICEF ambassador for Serbia, he helps raise the awareness of low enrollment rates in preschool education in his native country, which are among the lowest in the world.

Through the accomplishments of Ivanovic and Djokovic—talented athletes, advocates, and philanthropists—their countrymen and -women see that even the impossible is possible. Their success, driven by their focus and spirit, inspires others to believe that they can also overcome seemingly insurmountable circumstances. It allows them not only to have hopes and dreams, but to aspire to them. Ivanovic and Djokovic have also made great strides to help redeem their country in the eyes of the world after it was tainted by atrocities and war crimes.

The swimming pool alumni Ivanovic and Djokovic were cheered by a crowd of 15,000 when they returned to Belgrade from the French Open in 2007. They both made the semifinals at the Grand Slam. They had earned every one of those cheers. Their journey has been a testament to the strength of will and purpose of fierce competitors who did not let circumstances define them, who instead defined themselves, and in so doing, redefined their country. They showed the tenacity of their people, who have survived years of conflict and stigma, and will not be defined by them.

YOU RUN LIKE A GIRL

Gender Biases in Sports

*My coach said I ran like a girl. I said if he could
run a little faster, he could too.*
—MIA HAMM

Women have certainly come a long way. "Running like a girl" used to be a slur, but now it can mean being as fierce on the soccer field as Mia Hamm. Today, "hitting like a girl" can mean being a knockout powerhouse like the mixed martial arts fighter Amanda Nunes. Nunes stunned the crowd when she defeated the equally intimidating Ronda Rousey in a first-round ten-second knockout at UFC 207 in December 2016.

Historically, women's sports and the role of women in

sports have been defined and ultimately shaped by men, by their personal values and (mis)understanding of how men and women should look, act, and be perceived based on their gender. At times these biases have led to women being excluded from sports completely or prejudgments of what female athletes were capable of, and even how they should look.

Sports began as a curriculum that was exclusively for boys and men. It was seen as an outlet for energetic boys and a way to create a masculine environment to bond, nurture sportsmanship, and create friendships. To that end, sports was incorporated into school curriculums by men, for men, and was geared to men, as a celebration of masculinity, strength, and the competitive spirit. When we look at how sports and subsequently the perception of the athlete has evolved, it is no wonder that women were excluded by default by sport's very definition, framework, and parameters. Even the sports philosophies between men and women were markedly different. For women, the sports culture emphasized pleasure and social competition, with the ultimate goal being self-development and teamwork, as opposed to the male sports culture of winning, machismo, bravado, and being the best.

Sports, and its evolution, have had historic and existing biases, and also a sports culture that nurtures and sustains them. In the 1900s, doctors thought that physical activity would damage women's reproductive systems and also create muscles, which at that time were considered unattractive on women. Because of these misconceptions and seemingly personal biases, women's participation in sports was limited to more feminine activities like archery, dancing, tennis, croquet, golf, and swimming. As recently as just 1972, the longest race women were allowed in was the 1,500 meter, because of nineteenth-century beliefs that women could not mentally or physically cope with longer events. Luckily, we know today that there are no medical, physical, or mental reasons that restrict women or girls from competing in sports, yet many biases, such as appearance, the competitive spirit, and perceptions of masculinity and femininity, remain as holdovers from this outdated mentality.

Many of these physical, emotional, and psychological myths were less supported by medical facts than by stereotypically masculine values and ideals, which considered women in sports as incompatible with the role of women in society. Because of that mode of thinking—and there is still evidence of much-needed change—women who were overly competitive were stigmatized as being unfeminine and even masculine.

In 1971, the Association for Intercollegiate Athletics for Women (AIAW) was created by female physical educators as a "model of athletic governance designed for female student-athletes, which incorporated the prevailing women's sports philosophy."[1] Shortly after, in 1972, Congress enacted Title IX of the Education Amendments. A federal civil rights statute, the title states: "No person in the United States shall, on the basis of sex, be excluded from participation in, be denied the benefits of, or be subjected to discrimination under any education program or activity receiving Federal financial assistance."[2]

The AIAW was founded because at that time sports scholarships were not offered to women, creating a disparity between male and female athletes. It would also, according to a 1996 study by M. J. Festle, "help schools extend their sports programs for women . . . stimulate leadership among those (mostly women) who were responsible for women's programs . . . [and conduct] national athletic championships for women."[3]

"The AIAW was a small organization with a limited budget. Unlike the National Collegiate Athletic Association (NCAA), and the National Association of Intercollegiate Athletics (NAIA), both originally men's sport governing organizations, the AIAW made no distinction between revenue and non-revenue sports. In fact, fearing that with money came corruption and exploitation, it wasn't until the latter part of 1973, in response to legal pressures associated with Title IX compliance, that the AIAW allowed women who accepted athletic scholarships to compete in its national championships."[4]

"During the 1972–73 season, the AIAW offered its first seven national championships (badminton, basketball, golf, gymnastics, swimming & diving, track & field, and volleyball), and by the 1980–81 season the AIAW national program had grown to 39 championships in 17 different sports with 6,000 women's teams and 960 member institutions."[5]

Title IX affected sport-specific opportunities for women and girls as well as the ongoing evolution of school sport governance. The law meant that "institutions could not discriminate on the basis of gender, in any program receiving federal funds, including athletics."[6] According to Indiana Democratic senator Birch Bayh, the principal Senate sponsor of Title IX, the act was put forth as "a strong and comprehensive measure [that would] provide women with solid legal protection from the persistent, pernicious discrimination which is serving to perpetuate second-class citizenship for American women."[7]

In other words, Title IX made it a requirement under law

for male and female students to be afforded equal federal funding in their high school and college studies. Before that, young women could not get an athletic scholarship in the States. Because of Title IX, women from all over the world can go to American colleges on a scholarship and get grants. This meant that women had the same opportunities as men, and it created equality in education and sports activities. As noted by Robert Everhart and Cynthia Lee Pemberton in *The Institutionalization of a Gender-Biased Sport Value System*:

> Historically and traditionally sport has evolved as a male domain, and it is clear that women and girls, as well as men and boys, have different sport participation roots. The evidence presented supports the notion that gender bias in sport is a product of not only different sport histories and traditions, but also an inherent incompatibility between female and male sport cultures and values. The dominant male sport value system has defined and delimited the parameters of sport for women and girls, especially and ironically since the passage of Title IX. Further, evidence has been presented to show that gender bias and gender discrimination are manifest in sport through differences in both the quantity and quality of the sport experiences/programs available, as well as the virtual elimination of female sport administrative leadership and dramatically reduced numbers of female sport coaches.
>
> The apparent physical, mental, emotional, and socio-cultural benefits of sport participation, have been, until recently, largely denied to women and girls. Given these

contextual realities it isn't surprising that as yet women and girls don't participate in school sport to the same degree men and boys do. It's surprising that given the long history of gender bias and discrimination, the many ways bias and discrimination have been institutionalized through male dominated norms and values, the operational structures and component parts that facilitate and/or delimit female school sport participation, and a differential valuing of the male/female sport experience, that women and girls participate in sport to the degree that they do. The question isn't how come things are as they are. The question is how could they be otherwise?[8]

Public Perception
of Female Athletes

Body 1

Although today women have competed in and found success in almost every area of the male-dominated world of sports, they continue to struggle for balance, and at times acceptance, within a sport model founded on the outmoded and antiquated characterization of women as the weaker sex, and of strong competitive women as unfeminine and unattractively masculine. Though not as wide-ranging as the perception of women as the weaker sex (a myth shattered by Billie Jean King), this outdated notion of men and women as not being equal has often formed a baseline for standards and the criteria for how achievements are measured, how systems are created, and even how whole organizations are founded or structured.

Although it is not as overt as in the 1900s, when doctors thought that physical activity would endanger women's reproductive systems and also create "unsightly" muscles, outdated conceptions of women are still prevalent in sports today. Now they distinguish themselves in different, less overt, more subtle ways. For instance, such attitudes manifest themselves in the social expectations of male and female athletes, how they should look and act, and also in inequitable prize money and endorsement deals. Let's take, for instance, Venus and Serena Williams.

The unapologetic physicality and sheer prowess of trailblazers like Billie Jean King, Martina Navratilova, and Venus and Serena Williams debunked the stereotypes of how women play or *should* play tennis, and how they should look while doing it. When you combine these accomplishments with their activism—King for gender equality, Navratilova for gay rights and marriage equality, and the Williams sisters for equal prize money and women's advocacy—they have not only changed the perception of female athletes on the court, they have also *literally* changed the game, and women's roles in sports and society.

The Williams sisters picked up a racket at three and four years old and have been a force in tennis ever since. Serena Williams has been working steadily for equality in endorsement monies with white female players. Despite being a top tennis player, Serena Williams was making $10 million less in endorsement money than Maria Sharapova, despite Sharapova's not being a real rival to Williams for years. Williams's endorsement deals exceeded Sharapova's only after Sharapova tested positive in a doping incident, after which she was banned from playing professional tennis for fifteen months. This gap may point to long-held prejudices regarding female sports stars and how fans (and advertisers and sponsors) feel they should look, or want them to look.

When the Williams sisters first hit the court, they were undeniably unlike any other female tennis players. They courted attention in not only their unorthodox and unapologetic tennis attire, and unabashed braided and beaded hairstyles, but also the sheer ferocity of their game. Though both tennis players, they are as different from each other as their game. Venus is tall, leggy, and lithe at 6'1". Venus plays gracefully but unemotionally. She is a focused, strategic, and composed baseline player, and a skilled volleyer with an attacking all-court game. She has the record for the fastest serve by a woman, clocked at 130 miles per hour at the Zurich Open.

Serena, at 5'9", is, I'll say it, a powerhouse, whose physicality dominates the game, her compact and muscular body belying her speed. Although not the most agile player, she more than makes up for it in—that's right—power. Just as focused on the court as her sister, Serena is outwardly more passionate, at times explosive in her reactions to what she believes are unfair calls or treatment. In the 2009 US Open semifinals, she threatened to make a line judge eat a tennis ball. At the 2016 Wimbledon center court finals, after dropping a tie against Christina McHale, she threw her racket so far it ended up in a cameraman's lap. That outburst cost her a $10,000 fine. Also a baseline player, she dominates rallies using her powerful serve and return and forceful ground strokes. Her wicked serve has been clocked at 128 miles per hour, and her slicing ace obliterates not only her opponents' return but also their composure. If that doesn't do it, her glares across the net are just as intimidating. Although the younger of these two immensely talented players, Serena has had a more successful tennis career. Not since Monica Seles's "unladylike" signature grunt had there been so much talk about appearance and decorum in women's tennis once Venus and Serena Williams arrived on the scene.

As a mixed-race athlete in a sport perceived as white, I understand and have faced the challenges of always having to prove yourself and being judged as "that one" or of standing out because of the way you look. To add in being a woman and having to fight the uphill battle of proving yourself for your race and gender is an unimaginable burden. To have to go out on the court and play well, bearing that pressure on your shoulders, is an almost herculean task. That Williams has had only a few of those incidents of lashing out is to me an accomplishment, perhaps even commendable. Players, many not even under the microscopic lens of race and gender, have outbursts all the time. And most would not be able to survive on tour for a year, let alone twenty-one years, dealing with that kind of pressure.

At thirty-five, Williams reached three Grand Slam finals and began now taking stock of her athletic career and her life. She won the Australian Open in 2017 against her thirty-six-year-old sister, Venus. This is another example of the Williams sisters breaking the mold because of their continued accomplishments at an age when most players are hanging up their rackets, and also how long their careers have lasted. During an interview in December 2016 with the rapper Common for ESPN's blog *The Undefeated,* Common asked, "As we talk about black people being marginalized and women being marginalized, do you think it's ironic that a black woman is in the conversation as the greatest athlete ever?" Williams replied, "I think if I were a man, I would have been in that conversation a long time ago. I think being a woman is just a whole new set of problems from society that you have to deal with, as well as being black, so it's a lot to deal with—and especially lately. I've been able to speak up for women's rights because I think that gets lost in color, or gets lost in cultures. Women make up so much of this world, and, yeah, if I were a man, I would have 100 percent been considered the greatest ever a long time ago."

It is hard to argue with her when you look at her accomplishments: she has won twenty-three Grand Slam singles titles (which breaks Steffi Graf's Open-era record), and thirteen doubles titles, two mixed doubles, and four Olympic gold medals. Yet when it comes to prize money, she trails behind male tennis players, and until recently she made less money in endorsement deals than female tennis players such as Maria Sharapova who are no real threat to her on the court. *Rolling Stone* wrote in July 2013, "Here are the facts. Serena is the number-one tennis player in the world. Maria Sharapova is the number-two tennis player in the world. Sharapova is tall, white and blond, and, because of that, makes more money in endorsements than Serena, who is black, beautiful and built like one of those monster trucks that crushes Volkswagens at sports arenas. Sharapova has not beaten Serena in nine years."

When we factor in the media scrutiny about her body, her commanding presence on the courts, the vivacious colors and style of her tennis outfits, and her riotous, untamed hair, we have to wonder about this disparity. Considering the outmoded societal expectations and perceptions of female athletes, it is undeniable that Serena Williams has shattered ex-

pectations of what a female tennis player should look like and
how she should also play.

When asked about how she felt about the media's public
scrutiny of her body, Williams answered, "There was a time
when I didn't feel incredibly comfortable about my body because I felt like I was too strong. I had to take a second and
think, 'Who says I'm too strong?' This body has enabled me
to be the greatest player that I can be. And now my body is in
style, so I'm feeling good about it. I'm just really thankful for
the way I was brought up by my mom and my dad to give me
that confidence. I could have been discouraged, and I wouldn't
be as great as I was because I would have done different exer-
cises or I would have done different things. I totally embrace
who I am and what I am."

In closing out a turbulent 2016, marked by great achievements and I can imagine even greater lessons, Williams reached
the finals of three Grand Slam events, winning Wimbledon.
She lost in a US Open semifinal. In an open letter in *Porter*
magazine's Incredible Women of 2016 issue, Williams took
aim at the barriers that still hold female athletes back. She
addressed it to all incredible women who strive for excellence.

> When I was growing up, I had a dream . . . my dream
> was to be the best tennis player in the world. Not the
> best "female" tennis player in the world. . . . What oth-
> ers marked as flaws or disadvantages about myself—my
> race, my gender—I embraced as fuel for my success. . . .
> Women have to break down many barriers on the road
> to success. One of those barriers is the way we are con-
> stantly reminded we are not men, as if it is a flaw. People

call me one of the "world's greatest female athletes." Do they say LeBron is one of the world's best male athletes? Is Tiger? Federer? . . . We should always be judged by our achievements, not by our gender. We must continue to dream big, and in doing so, we empower the next generation of women to be just as bold in their pursuits.

The Williams sisters' goal of being at the top of their sport is clearly not nearly enough. While Serena advocates for women's rights, Venus has championed equal pay for women since 1998, when she made her first public mention about equal prize money to men and women after a first-round Wimbledon match.

The prize money on the WTA Tour is not equal to the prize money given to men. The WTA does not give equal prize money at all the events because they are two different tours. They give equal prize money at the slams when the men and women are together at the same event. But then the tours split, and the sponsorship dollars are not the same. The main fight for equal prize money was around the Grand Slams, which were drastically unequal in Billie Jean King's era. She founded the WTT, which is a model for all the events counting equally with the men and women playing together. The US Open and Australian Open were the first to grant equal prize money to male and female champions, due to King's efforts. And it took decades for the French Open and Wimbledon to fall in line. They did not become equal until 2007, when Venus Williams finally helped to win equal prize money for female tennis players. And it was about time. At Wimbledon, one of the major Grand Slam events and among the oldest tennis tournaments in the sport's history, women had competed for less prize money than men since they began participating in 1880.

The significance of equal prize money is twofold. One, the women are now locked into any Grand Slam prize money increases that are granted to the men, which is a function of TV rights sales, ticket revenues, and sponsorships. There have been enormous increases in recent years. Two, there is a trickle-down effect wherein the non–Grand Slam events (the ATP and WTA Tours) will increase their prize money so that they are not left behind. There are also some combined non–Grand Slam events that have promised equal prize money in an effort to follow the Slams. Soccer is the current sport that is in a very similar space to the WTA and ATP before equal prize money. The US women's national soccer team is performing better at major events and is at a point where it should likely be paid the same as the men's team. That will be interesting to watch over the coming years.

But let's go back before Venus Williams won her battle for equal pay. In 2005, Williams beat Lindsay Davenport in the longest women's final in history and won the Wimbledon title. The day before the match, Williams attended a board meeting held by the All England Lawn Tennis and Croquet Club, the organization that runs the tournament, and asked everyone there to close their eyes and imagine being a little girl who trains for years only to "get to this stage, and you're told you're not the same as a boy."

That same year, Venus Williams won the women's championship game, collecting $1.08 million in prize money. Roger Federer won the men's championship and collected $1.13 million in prize money. Several months after Williams's speech at the All England Club, the women's championship prize money was increased, but it still did not match the men's award. The club chairman, Tim Phillips, justified the prize discrepancy by saying that the physical demands of the men's best-of-five matches are much higher than those of the women's best-of-three. Phillips added that the club didn't view the prize discrepancy as "an equal rights issue," and he also noted that "the top ten ladies last year earned more from Wimbledon than the top ten men did" by also playing in the doubles tournament.

Williams's long and winding road to equal prize money finally culminated in 2006 when she wrote an op-ed in the *Times of London* calling for Wimbledon to pay men and women athletes equally. In it, Williams argued that Wimbledon's prize structure "devalues the principle of meritocracy and diminishes the years of hard work that women on the tour have put into becoming professional tennis players. The message I like to convey to women and girls across the globe is that there is no glass ceiling. My fear is that Wimbledon is loudly and clearly sending the opposite message." The piece generated enough attention from British politicians that then-MP Janet Anderson brought it up during a question-and-answer session in Parliament, prompting Prime Minister Tony Blair to endorse equal pay in his response.

In 2007, Williams's efforts finally paid off. A statement from Chairman Phillips read, "This year, taking into account both the overall progression and the fact that broader social factors are also relevant to the decision, they [the Committee] have decided that the time is right to bring this subject to a logical conclusion and eliminate the difference."

After Venus heard about this decision, she responded with

her own statement: "The greatest tennis tournament in the world has reached an even greater height today. I applaud today's decision by Wimbledon, which recognizes the value of women's tennis."

That year, Venus Williams won her fourth Wimbledon singles title and was paid the same as the men's winner, Roger Federer. By speaking out for equal prize money for women, Venus Williams, with support from Serena Williams, Jennifer Capriati, Maria Sharapova, Kim Clijsters, and Petra Kvitova, was able to win equal pay for female players. She also changed the way female tennis players are valued. To fully understand the difference achieving equal prize money made for female athletes, consider that Serena Williams's earnings the year after women achieved equal prize money in 2007 was an impressive $12 million or more. This shows the impact of equal prize money financially for female athletes.

When young girls watch the Williams sisters on the court, or see them in commercials or as spokespeople for one of their many business ventures, they know that despite their own appearance or socioeconomic backgrounds, they can be the best at anything they set out to do. All they need is the drive to be the best, and the strength of character to not care about what society, in its outmoded ideologies, may think.

Billie Jean King and the Original Nine players in the newly conceived WTA opened the door to pay equality. Venus Williams and a new generation of superstars, Kim Clijsters, Justine Henin, Jennifer Capriati, Martina Hingis, Serena Williams, Mary Pierce, Monica Seles, Anna Kournikova, Maria Sharapova, and Lindsay Davenport among them, kicked the door down. Capitalizing on King's original fight to introduce the concept of equal prize money, the WTA leadership, led by Larry Scott, its CEO, made a business case to demonstrate that the women were on par in terms of the business metrics (match viewership, attendance, sponsorship interest, and so forth). This wave happened during the postretirement period of Andre Agassi and Pete Sampras, when the women's matches were often more commercially interesting than the men's matches. For example, Venus or Serena have historically outrated almost any other match (male or female) on ESPN to this day. Sharapova, Serena, Venus, and other female players generated more endorsement income individually than almost all the men at that time. Women's soccer should be next if it follows this model.

SHUT UP AND PLAY

*The Impetus and Social Ramifications
of Sports Activism*

lthough not comparable to the hardships athletes faced for advocating for equality and human rights during the civil rights era, the challenges faced by sports activists today still constitute no small feat. The ramifications of sports activism today differ significantly from those in the past on many levels, because the sports world is now so vastly different, with a myriad of personal, familial, societal, and financial considerations. These days, professional athletes have to take into account corporate relationships, sponsorships, and endorsements as much as their fans' response to their activism. Athletes also have varying considerations depending on their sport. Team-sport athletes face different challenges than individual-sport athletes. As a tennis player, I do have to consider how my actions may affect my corporate sponsors and endorsements, but not how they will affect my team or my teammates. However, if the basketball superstar LeBron James decides to endorse a candidate for president, he must take into account the potentially detrimental effect it could have on his Cleveland Cavaliers teammates, on the sponsorship and endorsement deals for the franchise, and on the Cavaliers' dedicated and highly vocal fans.

Today's sports stars are stellar athletes at the top of their form who are functioning at unbelievable physical and mental levels. But the career of an athlete, depending on the sport, tends to be short. Football players have about three years at the top of their field to make enough money to be able to sustain themselves and their families and to achieve financial security before they leave the game. For baseball players it is a little longer depending on the player and the team. Hockey players, in their fast-moving and volatile sport, are always in danger of injury. Team players can be traded without notice, and their life, and their family's life, can be turned upside down if they are forced to move across the country, or if they become free agents but are not signed to a team right away, or at all.

The ramifications of activism in today's sponsor- and endorsement-fueled sports world, the backlash from the community of superfans, and the cultural stereotypes of professional athletes as dumb jocks who should just "shut up and play" create hardships and consequences that should not and cannot be underestimated. They are wide-ranging and extend far from the playing field into our personal lives, and we have to consider our fans, our sport, and our brand, team, and franchise identity. At the end of the day, when the stadium lights dim and our careers come to an end, we will still have to be able to support our families. This is made even more difficult because professional athletes do not always have a fallback plan, advanced degrees, or skills that are easily transferable from the field, ice, or court, because we have spent most of our lives training our body and mind for our sport.

When an athlete protests or speaks out for a cause, he or she fully understands the ramifications. In today's sports world we have to; it is part and parcel of playing the game. It is often surprising what athletes have to take into consideration because they play professional sports. When I decided, at the height of my tennis career, to cut my dreadlocks, my agent warned me that I would be losing millions of dollars in endorsement deals. To think: something as seemingly inconsequential and personal as cutting my hair would have such serious financial consequences, which could affect my family.

In 2012 LeBron James, Dwyane Wade, and several of their Miami Heat teammates wore hoodies before a game against the Detroit Pistons to protest the killing of Trayvon Martin and police brutality, knowing that they would face fines and fan backlash. James also wrote "Trayvon Martin RIP" on his sneaker to honor the African American teen who was shot to death by George Zimmerman, a neighborhood watch volunteer and German Peruvian who has been called "white" and "white Hispanic" in the media. Several members of the Heat posed together for a photo in the hooded sweatshirts. Their heads were bowed and their faces hidden in their hoods. Their message could be interpreted as meaning that off the court, in a hoodie, they could all be Trayvon Martin. James posted the photo on social media. The image—shared around the world—made the Heat the most prominent collection of athletes to protest Martin's death. They were dedicated to the cause even in the face of a several-game suspension.

LeBron James, the greatest player in basketball by far, does not often get commended or recognized for his advocacy, activism, and philanthropy. One of the most well-known athletes in the world right now, he fully endorsed Hillary Clinton during her 2016 campaign, despite what could have been considerable repercussions and at a time when few athletes were public about the candidate they supported. James even went on to make a stump speech for Clinton. He has also donated a significant amount of his own money to effect change in the country. Specifically, he has given $40 million to fund scholarships in his hometown of Akron. His is the first generation of athletes who are financially in a position to make these types of contributions, which is very different from the athletes of the 1960s. So while James wore the hoodie and later spoke out at the ESPYs, as an act of activism, he is also making tangible, far-reaching efforts to address social issues and implement social change.

How James and other superstar athletes like Colin Kaepernick, who donated $1 million to communities in need and is donating $100,000 a month for a year to different local community groups, choose to financially augment their activism, often with an enormous amount of wealth invested into communities, to address social disparity, illustrates how many of today's modern athletes practice activism. Many athletes are criticized for doing the PR part but not the real work behind the scenes. These types of financial commitment show a heightened level of dedication that is distinct from many others and can be considered real action.

James continues to speak out on issues that are important to him, regardless of backlash. His approach may be different from Colin Kaepernick's steady approach, or Chris Kluwe's steadfast and outspoken one, but sports activism in today's corporate franchise environment is, first and foremost, a personal choice, which warrants an individualized approach. It is not for everyone, and what matters is not the impetus, the timing, or the steps taken, but only that the athlete walks the road best for him or her, while still being able to succeed in and love the game he or she has worked so hard to be able to play professionally.

Dedication and Determination

Professional athletes can become a conduit through which the sports community can work to unite people to create solutions that will improve race and gender relations. Athletes and the sports community as a whole have been critical components of bringing people together to fight inequality. They can be a crucial element to healing our nation right now at a very divisive moment in our history. Their actions have helped achieve social justice, historically and today.

A Super Bowl champion and a three-time NFL Pro Bowler, Brendon Ayanbadejo, a former linebacker for the Baltimore Ravens, has been an outspoken advocate of gay rights and a champion of marriage equality since 2009. Born to an Irish American mother and a Nigerian father, he grew up determined to make a difference by fighting bias and discrimination.

To Ayanbadejo, the fight to legalize same-sex marriage is the twenty-first-century version of the fight for racial equality. He has publicly announced that, as the son of interracial parents whose own marriage would have been illegal in sixteen states prior to the US Supreme Court's landmark *Loving v. Virginia* decision in 1967, he had no intention of remaining silent on an issue of conscience and public importance.

Ayanbadejo's advocacy is wide-ranging and seemingly tireless. He has posed with his family and other NFL members of Athlete Ally for the NOH8 (No Hate) photo campaign shot by Adam Bouska. Ayanbadejo was also a guest editor of the *Washington Blade*'s special August 2013 LGBT sports edition. In 2009, he wrote an article for the *Huffington Post* titled "Same-Sex Marriages: What's the Big Deal?" In the piece, he suggested a separation of church and state in creating policy. "First and foremost," he wrote, "church and state are supposed to be completely separated when it comes to the rule of law in the United States. So the religious argument that God meant for only man and woman to be together has no bearing here! . . . Maybe I am a man ahead of my time. However, looking at the former restrictions on human rights in our country starting with slavery, women not being able to vote, blacks being counted as two-thirds [historically three-fifths] of a human, segregation, no gays in the military (to list a few) all have gone by the wayside. But now here in 2009 same sex marriages are prohibited. I think we will look back in 10, 20, 30 years and be amazed that gays and lesbians did not have the same rights as everyone else. How did this ever happen in the land of the free and the home of the brave? Are we really free?"

Founded in 2008, NOH8 was originally formed in response

to California's Proposition 8, a statewide ballot proposition that in 2008 made same-sex marriage illegal in California. In 2013, to counter homophobic comments about gay players in the NFL and to raise awareness for marriage equality and gay rights, Ayanbadejo decided to showcase many of the athletes who support NOH8. Ayanbadejo and Athlete Ally arranged a photo campaign with NOH8, which he and his family also posed for. In the campaign, Ayanbadejo wanted to show that there are NFL players who proudly support equal rights. A few athletes who were photographed in support of the campaign were the former Minnesota Vikings punter Chris Kluwe, the New York Jets cornerback Antonio Cromartie and safety Bret Lockett, the Carolina Panthers linebacker Nic Harris, the Saint Louis Rams defensive tackle Matt Willig, and Athlete Ally's founder, Hudson Taylor, a three-time All-American wrestler.

Chris Kluwe is also a staunch and very outspoken advocate for marriage equality. Kluwe, a supporter of Minnesotans for Equality, actively campaigned against Minnesota's Amendment 1 in 2012, which would have defined marriage as a union between one man and one woman. Kluwe's activism even landed him on the cover of *Out* magazine that year. In 2012, Ayanbadejo supported a Maryland ballot initiative to legalize same-sex marriage in the state, which passed, albeit with a narrow margin. His public support drew ire from Maryland Democratic state delegate Emmett C. Burns Jr., who wrote a letter to the Baltimore Ravens expressing his dismay that Ayanbadejo was voicing his support for same-sex marriage.

In the letter addressed to the Ravens' owner, Steve Bisciotti, Burns wrote, "I find it inconceivable that one of your players, Mr. Brendon Ayanbadejo, would publicly endorse Same-Sex marriage, specifically as a Ravens football player." According to WBAL-TV, Burns became upset when he learned that Ayanbadejo had contributed a pair of Ravens tickets to a fundraiser for Marylanders for Marriage Equality. After expressing his dismay at Ayanbadejo's actions in his letter, Burns then asked the Ravens to silence the football veteran. "I am requesting that you take the necessary action, as a National Football League Owner, to inhibit such expressions from your employees and that he be ordered to cease and desist such injurious actions. I know of no other NFL player who has done what Mr. Ayanbadejo is doing."

Defending Ayanbadejo, Kluwe shot back in an open letter, saying that perhaps Burns did not have an understanding of the Constitution, since the "very first amendment deals with the freedom of speech, particularly the abridgment of said freedom." An excerpt from his letter, published in the *Huffington Post*, reads:

> I can assure you that gay people getting married will have zero effect on your life. They won't come into your house and steal your children. They won't magically turn you into a lustful cockmonster. They won't even overthrow the government in an orgy of hedonistic debauchery because all of a sudden they have the same legal rights as the other 90 percent of our population, rights like Social Security benefits, childcare tax credits, family and medical leave to take care of loved ones, and COBRA health care for spouses and children. You know what having these rights will make gay Americans? Full-fledged citizens, just like everyone else, with the freedom to pursue

happiness and all that that entails. Do the civil-rights struggles of the past 200 years mean absolutely nothing to you?

At first Burns, who is also the pastor and founder of the Rising Sun First Baptist Church in Woodlawn, Maryland, defended his letter, but a few days later in a weekend phone interview with the *Baltimore Sun*, Burns relented: "Upon reflection, [Ayanbadejo] has his First Amendment rights. And I have my First Amendment rights. . . . Each of us has the right to speak our opinions. The football player and I have a right to speak our minds."

This is a powerful example of activism in action because of its almost immediate effect. For Kluwe to persuade such an influential figure to *publicly* admit that Ayanbadejo has his right to speak his opinion, and to his opinion, is an important first step. I highly doubt that Burns's feelings on gay marriage have completely changed, but to me this is progress because his public response could sway others. To me, considering Burns's station as a state representative, it seems to fly in the face of human rights and equality in a country that was built on those tenets, that this much progress is needed to grant another member of the human race equal rights. His actions are unconscionable and self-defeating. This is another reason why activists have a necessary role in today's society, and what they can do when they are stalwart, informed, and dedicated.

In April 2016, Ayanbadejo, the *Sports Illustrated* Sports Activist of the Year, along with Kluwe and the New Orleans Saints linebacker Scott Fujita, filed a voluntary brief with the Supreme Court in support of plaintiffs challenging bans on gay marriage. The brief mentioned the NBA center Jason Collins and the NFL free agent Michael Sam, the first openly gay players in the NBA and NFL, and their struggle to be accepted by their teams, their fans, and the media.

Collins, who has played for six pro teams and in two NBA Finals, came out as gay in 2013 and Michael Sam in 2014. In *Sports Illustrated*, Collins wrote, "I didn't set out to be the first openly gay athlete playing in a major American team sport. But since I am, I'm happy to start the conversation. I wish I wasn't the kid in the classroom raising his hand and saying, 'I'm different.' If I had my way, someone else would have already done this. Nobody has, which is why I'm raising my hand."

In elaborating on why he was coming out at that time, he wrote, "Now I'm a free agent, literally and figuratively. I've reached that enviable state in life in which I can do pretty much what I want. And what I want is to continue to play basketball. I still love the game, and I still have something to offer. My coaches and teammates recognize that. At the same time, I want to be genuine and authentic and truthful."

"I am not the only gay person in the NFL," Sam said during a speech and Q&A session in Dallas in 2015, according to the *Fort Worth Star-Telegram*. "I'm just saying there is a lot of us. I respect the players that did reach out to me and had the courage to tell me that they were also gay, but they do not have the same courage as I do to come out before I even played a down in the NFL. Was it a risky move? Yes. But at that moment, the reason why I came out is I thought it wasn't going to be a big deal. Maybe I was naive. Maybe I thought it was

2014, and people will understand that there's gay NFL players. There's gay athletes everywhere. But I was clearly wrong. It was a huge deal."

Both Sam and Collins were praised by President Obama and their journeys as openly gay athletes dominated sports coverage. Before retiring in 2015, Collins played thirteen seasons in the NBA. He played for the New Jersey Nets, the Memphis Grizzlies, the Minnesota Timberwolves, the Atlanta Hawks, the Boston Celtics, and the Washington Wizards. After the 2012–13 NBA season ended, Collins publicly came out as gay. He became a free agent and did not play again until February 2014, when he signed with the Brooklyn Nets and became the first publicly gay athlete to play in any of the four major North American pro sports leagues. In April 2014, Collins was featured on the cover of *Time* magazine as one of the one hundred most influential people in the world.

Michael Sam publicly came out as gay after completing his college football career. He became the first publicly gay player to be drafted in the NFL. Sam's draft stock never recovered after he came out. He went through training camp with the Saint Louis Rams and appeared in all four preseason games. Sam was one of the last cuts by the team despite his notable performance. He was finally signed by the Dallas Cowboys, where he lasted until October, when he was released. He found a home with the Montreal Alouettes before the 2015 season, and became the first publicly gay player to play in the Canadian Football League (CFL). Since Michael Sam came out, no other professional male athlete has made the decision to do so. We have to wonder how an athlete as talented as Sam, the

2013 SEC co-defensive player of the year, took so long to find a permanent home with a team, or why no other athlete in the NFL has come out as gay since Sam.

In their Supreme Court brief, Ayanbadejo, Fujita, and Kluwe draw a parallel between homophobia in professional sports and the fight for civil rights and equality. "Is it really too hard to see the parallels between this and what people said of Jackie Robinson almost 70 years ago?" the brief states. "Jackie Robinson was a singular athlete and singular man, but the slurs hurled against him sprang from the same place as the slurs hurled against Michael Sam. They are illegitimate views, wrongly motivated, and used to take equal rights away from the minority. They led this Court to apply the Constitution properly in the area of race a half-century ago, and they should lead to proper application of the Constitution again today."

Kluwe's and Ayanbadejo's support of the It Gets Better Project has made a difference to the upcoming generation of young people fighting discrimination and homophobia. The It Gets Better campaign reaches out to lesbian, gay, bisexual, and transgender youth around the world to show support of their journey and to let them know that it will get better. The project started in 2010 when the author and syndicated columnist Dan Savage created a YouTube video with his partner, Terry Miller, to inspire hope for young people facing harassment and bullying, particularly in the wake of young gay students taking their lives because of bullying in school. The movement has inspired more than fifty thousand user-created videos, which have been viewed more than fifty million times. The organization has received video submissions from celebrities, politicians, athletes, and activists, among them Barack

Obama, Hillary Clinton, Ellen DeGeneres, Anne Hathaway, and Colin Farrell, as well as members of the Broadway and media communities.

In 2011, the San Francisco Giants became the first MLB team to make an It Gets Better video. Shortly after the Giants' video was released, the Baltimore Orioles became the second Major League Baseball team to join the It Gets Better campaign. In August 2012, the San Francisco 49ers became the first NFL team to participate in the program.

The Backlash of Sports Activism

Chris Kluwe and Brendon Ayanbadejo are undeniably ardent supporters of gay rights and marriage equality. The advocacy of these determined activist athletes is undoubtedly making a difference in the world, but at what personal cost? Always outspoken, Kluwe wrote a *Deadspin* column in 2014 titled "I Was an NFL Player Until I Was Fired by Two Cowards and a Bigot." Kluwe believes his continued support of same-sex marriage and marriage equality contributed to the Vikings' decision to cut him after the 2012 season. He also believes this is why, despite still having the physical ability to compete in the NFL, he has not found a place on another team. "I can still hit the ball 45 yards outside the numbers with good hangtime, and at the tryouts I've had this year I've gotten praise from the scouts and personnel people on hand, but for whatever reason I cannot find a job."[1]

Kluwe thinks that no matter how much he wants to prove he can play, he will no longer punt in the NFL. Whether it's his age, his minimum veteran salary, his habit of speaking his mind, or a combination of all three, he believes his time as a football player is over. "Punters are always replaceable, at least in the minds of those in charge, and I realize that in advocating noisily for social change I only made it easier for them to justify not having me around. Some will ask if the NFL has a problem with institutionalized homophobia. I don't think it does. I think there are homophobic people in the NFL, in all positions, but that's true for society as well, and those people eventually get replaced. All we can do is try to expose their behavior when we see it and call them to account for their actions."[2]

Kluwe believes in his cause so strongly that he brought a lawsuit against the Minnesota Vikings in 2014 following his release from the team in May 2013, which he is convinced was due to his continued support of marriage equality and gay rights. The suit initially sought damages of $1 million to Kluwe, who would donate it to LGBT causes. The parties settled for an undisclosed amount, which the Vikings agreed to donate directly to five LGBT organizations, with Kluwe agreeing to receive nothing.

Clayton Halunen, Kluwe's lawyer, announced at a media conference that "the lawsuit will allege religious discrimination, sexual orientation discrimination, defamation and tortious interference with contractual obligations, resulting in Kluwe's release from the team in May 2013 after what he says was a pattern of intolerant language by special teams coordinator Mike Priefer related to Kluwe's activism on gay marriage."[3]

USA Today reported that "the Vikings retained former Minnesota Supreme Court justice Eric Magnuson and former U.S. Department of Justice trial attorney Chris Madel to complete what it called an independent review of the matter Jan. 3, the same day Kluwe made his allegations in a Deadspin.com post."[4]

The lawsuit was in response to the review, which Kluwe wanted to be made public. The media conference was called after Halunen received word from the Vikings that they had "no intent" to release the report to Kluwe or to the public. Kluwe and the Vikings reached a settlement the following August. Kluwe called the settlement an opportunity "to do a lot of good for a lot of people."

According to a report on ESPN.com, the Vikings and Kluwe's attorney Halunen announced that "they had reached a settlement to resolve the former punter's allegations of homophobic behavior by the team. It put the issue to rest 7½ months after Kluwe first published his allegations and avoids the prospect of a lengthy legal battle."[5]

The Vikings organization had initially announced a $100,000 contribution to lesbian, gay, bisexual, and transgender charities. They also plan to make additional contributions over the next five years. The team will also enhance sensitivity training that is already required throughout the organization.

At times, it seems that the leagues, the media, and the fans are more open to and accepting of damaging public missteps, or advocacy, if teams are producing on the court or field. For instance, the football star Ray Rice never got another chance in the league after he was filmed hitting and knocking out his fiancée. However, Greg Hardy, another pro football player, was given a second chance after his domestic violence case, I believe because his skills had not diminished the way Rice's had. I also think that it is likely Adrian Peterson would have no trouble getting back on an NFL roster after being convicted of child abuse because he is one of the best running backs in the league.

I am not advocating abuse in any way, just noting that these examples can set a precedent in regard to athletes deciding to speak out. I believe that no matter what Tom Brady or LeBron James says, because of their awesome abilities and sports prowess, there will always be a place for them on a roster. This gives them more leeway to speak their mind and not feel the same repercussions as someone like Kluwe. I am not saying that they have to speak up, but that they should understand that they have more freedom to do so. And if they do, the fallout will not be as detrimental.

Chris Kluwe and I are both members of Athlete Ally, an organization focused on ending homophobia and transphobia in sports by educating allies in the athletic community. I joined Athlete Ally after another former pro tennis player, Mardy Fish, told me about it. Mardy is a good friend. I was a groomsman at his wedding. When he was approached to join, he thought I might also be interested. I consider Mardy an activist athlete. Mardy suffered cardiac arrhythmia, also known as irregular heartbeat, in 2012. It led to a severe anxiety disorder that left him sometimes unable to leave his house. Since then he has been an advocate for those with mental illnesses like anxiety and depression, which, like everyone else, professional athletes also struggle with. High-profile athletes in football, soccer, tennis, and skiing have publicly discussed their experiences with depression, anxiety, stress, and panic attacks.

Chris Evert suffered from panic attacks after she stopped playing tennis. The New York Giants wide receiver Brandon

Tyrone Marshall works to raise awareness for mental health after being diagnosed with borderline personality disorder (BPD), a mental disorder characterized by unstable emotional moods. Although a part of the sports community, it is often not discussed because of the competitive nature of professional sports athletes, who always want to be perceived as being at the top of their game, mentally and physically.

I signed on with Athlete Ally as soon as I realized the good that the program does and how impassioned its founder, Hudson Taylor, is about the organization. During the Sochi Winter Olympics in 2014, Taylor advocated for LGBT rights and traveled to Sochi to speak out against the Russian law targeting LGBT citizens. The Anti-Gay Propaganda Law proposed by Russian president Vladimir Putin was signed into law in June 2013 and has prompted an increase in homophobic violence and hate crimes and numerous arrests of LGBT people in Russia. It has been widely referred to in the media as "one of the worst human rights violations in the post-Soviet era." Hudson gave his support to adding sexual orientation to the Olympic charter's antidiscrimination clause.

It was a thrill for me to get an award at the inaugural Athlete Ally Action Awards in 2014, in only my second year with the group. I was proud to be honored along with Yogi Berra, Jason Collins, and Martina Navratilova. I didn't realize what a difference my voice could make to help the LGBT community. It was an obvious decision. It seemed like the civil rights fights for African Americans of the generation previous. All LGBT people want is equal treatment under the law. At the very least there should not be laws that negatively target or affect them. That should not be too much to ask for. History shows how callous those who fought against equal rights are portrayed. I hope in the future that history will vindicate those who fought for equitable treatment for every person, no matter who they choose to love, and regardless of their gender or race.

Like Chris Kluwe and Brendon Ayanbadejo, I can make a difference as a straight athlete who is not afraid to stand up for LGBT rights. I think of the civil rights movement and the white people who stood with blacks against bigotry and discrimination. I want to show that it is not just an issue for the gay population to face alone, because it should matter to all people if anyone is being treated in an unfair or unjust way. As the son of a black father, I am committed to fighting discrimination in any form it may take. When I hear tragic stories about partners who have been together for over twenty years and are not allowed in the hospital room because their union is not recognized, my heart breaks, and it will never make sense to me. This is especially true because we live in a country founded on fighting for the rights of its individuals.

Since I have always held Chris Kluwe in high regard because of his advocacy, and since we are both members of Athlete Ally, I was excited when he agreed to talk to me about his activism and beliefs in human rights, especially after his highly publicized fallout with the Vikings. I greatly respected how he stood up for what he believed in regardless of whether it made him unpopular or its possible repercussions and consequences. Considering his outspokenness and his history, I was curious about his thoughts regarding sports franchises in general and about the role the public and management seems at times to want athletes to play. Chris did not have to think long about his answer.

"Based on my experiences, sports franchises have become heavily corporatized, and they only want their athletes to play the role of 'cog within the machine.' That means not speaking out on controversial issues, regardless of stance, and concealing who you are as a person in order to avoid offending anyone who might possibly buy a ticket or merchandise. I think this is a shame, because before we are athletes, we are human beings who are members of our society, and to ignore that in favor of a children's game is abdicating our responsibilities as citizens."

Although I was no longer playing professionally, my decision to advocate for more police conduct oversight and accountability after my incident in 2015 was something I gave a lot of consideration to. I wondered if Chris had thought about what he was possibly getting into as an advocate for marriage equality and LGBT rights and if becoming an activist was something he had been thinking about for a while, or if a situation presented itself that he couldn't ignore.

"For me, becoming an activist was something that just kind of presented itself. When an anti–same sex marriage amendment was proposed in Minnesota, an advocacy group asked me if I would get involved in helping to defeat it, and I said yes, since I don't think enshrining discrimination into a state's constitution is a particularly wise idea. Becoming an activist isn't something you have to spend months or years training to do, you just have to be willing to raise your voice when you have the platform and are in a position to help others.

"The hardest thing I think for anyone is making that initial decision. You have to weigh the potential consequences, like loss of employment, or physical injury, and then ask yourself if you're okay with the worst of those happening. If you decide you are, then go forward with no hesitation or regrets. In the end, if you can make the world a better place, in even the slightest way, it will have all been worth it."

When I asked Chris if there was anything he would have done differently, again he didn't pause. "I would have recorded all of my conversations in the Vikings facility once things started getting ugly between me and my special teams coach, Mike Priefer. For whatever reason, people have a hard time believing other people can do wretched things, and are willing to bend over backwards to accommodate the notion of doubt if it means someone they think shares their religious ideals might not be living up to those ideals. Having incontrovertible physical proof would have made the subsequent lawsuit much easier to fight, but unfortunately at the time, I did not know things were going to end the way they did. Hindsight is twenty-twenty, after all."

A Movement with Momentum

The issue of race and inequality in America played out over and over in the media and divided our nation in 2016. Shootings by police, bouts of discrimination, and divisive rhetoric and policy affect athletes in the same way they affect the wider society. Athletes using their platforms and their voices to create positive change often challenges people, fans, and the media because of the societal notion of the athlete and athletics. Many would like athletes to simply be entertainers. But we are not. We are human beings, we function within the wider society, and we are affected in many of the same ways. Since we have a greater reach and a louder, more meaningful voice, we want to use that voice on behalf of those who might not be as readily heard. However, as people in the public eye, we often find our actions to be misconstrued as ill informed or poorly executed.

The consequences of sports activism may be seen currently in the case of the former San Francisco 49ers quarterback Colin Kaepernick and his support of the Black Lives Matter movement. His peaceful protest has rippled far afield of the football stadium as it gained momentum, in sometimes surprising ways.

In August 2016, Steve Wyche from the NFL media saw Kaepernick sitting during the national anthem and asked him why. Kaepernick had done this for the previous two weeks, but nobody had noticed. His explanation was that he was protesting the oppression of black Americans. During the months that he continued not to stand for the anthem, America was experiencing what seemed like almost daily news reports and videos on social media of African American men, mostly unarmed men, being shot and killed by the police. In their wake, what started out as a fairly quiet demonstration gained substantial support and momentum. Since then the media attention and the subsequent backlash and support have also escalated.

Kaepernick sat during the anthem before a game against the Green Bay Packers at Levi's Stadium in California in August 2016. During the postgame interview, he announced his reason for not standing was that he does not want to "show pride in a flag for a country that oppresses black people and people of color. To me, this is bigger than football and it would be selfish on my part to look the other way. There are bodies in the street and people getting paid leave and getting away with murder."

After his announcement, the Niners coach, Chip Kelly, told reporters that Kaepernick's decision not to stand during the national anthem is "his right as a citizen" and said "it's not my right to tell him not to do something."

Kaepernick said that he was aware of what he is doing and that he knew it would not sit well with a lot of people. He did not inform the club or anyone affiliated with the team of his intentions to protest during the national anthem. "This is not something that I am going to run by anybody. I am not looking for approval. I have to stand up for people that are oppressed. . . . If they take football away, my endorsements from me, I know that I stood up for what is right."

Kaepernick thought about going public with his feelings for a while, but he wanted to better understand the situation. He discussed his concerns with his family and conferred with Dr. Harry Edwards, an activist and professor emeritus of sociology at the University of California. After months of witnessing some of the civil unrest in the United States, Kaepernick decided to be more active and involved in fighting for the rights of African Americans. Despite fan, media, and potential franchise backlash, he took a huge financial risk, even with a signed contract with the 49ers. After the 2016 season, the 49ers can cut him and not pay another cent of the deal he signed in 2014.

What is significant about his steady, peaceful approach is that it has legs. This is not a one-time incident that was talked about in a press conference and then forgotten. Since he began protesting every week during the games, his movement has gained momentum from athletes, fans, and the public supporting his cause, who are inspired by his dedication and steadfast approach.

Athletes across the country, professional, at the college level, and even in high schools, have joined Kaepernick in his protest. Four members of the Miami Dolphins kneeled on the ground during the anthem. After the game, the former running back Arian Foster said in an interview, "They say it's not the time to do this. When is the time? It's never the time in somebody else's eye, because they'll always feel like it's good enough. And some people don't." Kaepernick has gained support from high schoolers in Nebraska, Kentucky, Virginia, Illinois, Minnesota, and Maryland. The San Francisco 49ers safety Eric Reid, the New York Liberty guard Brittany Boyd, the Phoenix Mercury players Mistie Bass and Kelsey Bone, and the entire WNBA Indiana Fever team have kneeled with him. The list of athletes has further grown to include the Seattle Reign star Megan Rapinoe, the Denver Broncos linebacker Brandon Markeith Marshall, the Kansas City Chiefs' Marcus Peters, Martellus Bennett, and Devin McCourty of the New England Patriots, and it keeps growing.

Off the court, Kaepernick's support has grown across the country. Last October, a crowd of supporters showed up outside New Era Field in Orchard Park, Buffalo, and kneeled during the national anthem before the 49ers played the Bills. Some held up fists and others held signs showing support for Kaepernick and Black Lives Matter.

In Sacramento the day after the Sacramento Kings' NBA preseason game, the singer Leah Tysse took a knee as she sang the national anthem. She later explained why on social media. "I cannot idly stand by as black people are unlawfully profiled, harassed and killed by our law enforcement over and over and without a drop of accountability. The sad reality is, as a white American, I am bestowed a certain privilege in this nation that is not enjoyed by all people. Black families are having much different conversations with their children about how to interact with the police than white families."

While president, Barack Obama said that Kaepernick had been drawing attention to "some real, legitimate issues" and "exercising his constitutional right."

Kaepernick's protest has inspired football players and other athletes to speak up about race relations and police violence, and to do so in such a way that causes reporters, fans, and team owners actually to pay attention. As noted in *Slate*,

> According to Robert Klemko, more than 70 NFL players, including Kaepernick, Arian Foster, and Richard Sherman, are in a group text talking about "what Kaep started." That's not a gesture. That's a movement. . . .
>
> Just as important, Kaepernick has made his fellow Americans think about what they're standing for, and why. It wasn't typical for NFL players to stand for the national anthem until 2009—before then, it was customary for players to stay in the locker room as the anthem played. A 2015 congressional report revealed that the Department of Defense had paid $5.4 million to NFL teams between 2011 and 2014 to stage on-field patriotic ceremonies; the National Guard shelled out $6.7 million for similar displays between 2013 and 2015.[6]

The 49ers franchise announced it would donate $1 million to, in the words of the team's chief executive, Jed York, "the cause of improving racial and economic inequality and fostering communication and collaboration between law enforcement and the communities they serve here in the Bay Area." Kaepernick has pledged $1 million of his own money to address the same issues. "I have to help these people. I have to help these communities. It's not right that they're not put in a position to succeed or given those opportunities to succeed."

Reactions to Kaepernick were largely divided. Some applauded him for raising awareness about injustice and starting a nationwide discussion on race. Others saw his protest as unpatriotic, disrespectful to the flag and the country, and an offense not only to members of law enforcement but also to veterans and the military whose sacrifice and service the anthem honors.

Kaepernick has said many times that his "stance is not a criticism of the military and that he has great respect for the men and women who have fought for this country." And many vets support the spirit of his protest. Veterans and military members tweeted their support for him during this protest under the hashtag #VeteransForKaepernick. One such veteran, Nate Boyer, a former staff sergeant and Green Beret, wrote in an open letter to Kaepernick published in the *Army Times* in August 2016:

> I'm not judging you for standing up for what you believe in. It's your inalienable right. What you are doing takes a lot of courage, and I'd be lying if I said I knew what it was like to walk around in your shoes. I've never

had to deal with prejudice because of the color of my skin, and for me to say I can relate to what you've gone through is as ignorant as someone who's never been in a combat zone telling me they understand what it's like to go to war.

Even though my initial reaction to your protest was one of anger, I'm trying to listen to what you're saying and why you're doing it. When I told my mom about this article, she cautioned me that "the last thing our country needed right now was more hate." As usual, she's right.

There are already plenty of people fighting fire with fire, and it's just not helping anyone or anything. So I'm just going to keep listening, with an open mind. I look forward to the day you're inspired to once again stand during our national anthem. I'll be standing right there next to you. Keep on trying . . . De Oppresso Liber."[7]

Kaepernick invited Boyer to the 49ers September 1 game against the San Diego Chargers. And Boyer showed his support for the quarterback by standing next to him as the anthem played. Before the game, Boyer and Kaepernick talked for ninety minutes. A Twitter post featured a photo of the two men having what Boyer called a "good talk." He added, "Let's just keep moving forward. This is what America should be all about."

With the controversy came greater attention. In the first week of the regular season, just a few days after his initial protest, Kaepernick was featured on the cover of *Time* magazine, and his jersey became the biggest seller in the NFL. He also increased his number of followers on social media by about

18,000 per day at the height of the coverage of his protest in August and September. Kaepernick has also put his money where his mouth is by donating a million dollars to community organizations as well as all the profits from his jersey sales. This will instantly make a big difference in the communities that receive those funds. The power of substantial financial support through contributions and donations like these is one way today's athletes have as much power as, and perhaps even more than, sports activists in previous generations, because of today's sometimes massive contracts and sponsorships. In the past, athletes were not making huge amounts of money, so the protest itself was their only way to incite change.

It is worth noting that although many veterans support Kaepernick, there are still many others who feel that although they may appreciate his cause, the way he is protesting is disrespectful. I have to wonder that if he were kneeling to protest the twenty-three suicides per day that veterans commit, would the way he is protesting then be acceptable? Would the protest be okay if he were advocating for change in the way veterans are treated by the government after they return home from tours of duty? When I've asked these questions, the answer is almost always that protesting for those reasons would be okay, even admirable. Based on this, it appears that many people have an issue with the *subject* of the protest more than the *method* Kaepernick is using to protest. However, in the media, his method of not standing for the anthem is what is so often used as the target of attacks, which seems disingenuous and unfair when it could be argued that the real issue, that what seems to be making people uncomfortable, is the idea that racial inequality still exists in our country.

I want to show support for Kaepernick, but I also should point out, in fairness, that I do not agree with everything he has done as part of his protest. Protest does not have to be disrespectful or derogatory. I do not condone wearing socks that comically portray police officers as pigs. I did not condone kneeling during the moment of silence for victims of 9/11. And I definitely did not appreciate his statement that he didn't vote in the 2016 election. While voting is a freedom we are all afforded, and many have fought for, it is also our right not to vote. However, there were a few initiatives on the California ballot about capital punishment and police reform in 2016. If Kaepernick did not want to vote for the next president of the Unites States because he didn't like the choices, I can understand that, but there are also local issues in an election, in which one vote can make a huge difference. Part of any protest is what can be accomplished by it with actual progress. Voting can be a powerful way to incite change.

From Protest to Progress

I found out about the excellent work the Ross Initiative in Sports for Equality (RISE) is doing in educating collegiate and professional athletes to help inform and empower their activism when I was invited to participate in their focus group. Stephen Ross, the owner of the Miami Dolphins, founded RISE in 2015 in response to what he saw was a need for the sports community to come together to improve race relations.

RISE is an educational organization that recognizes the influential role that athletes have played throughout our country's history, by promoting better race relations and bringing the country together through sports. It is a collaboration among and a network of every sports league in the country. The board is composed of the commissioners of every professional sport as well as the presidents and CEOs of every sports network. They seek to harness the unifying power of sports to improve race relations. They bring athletes and organizations together to develop solutions to improve race relations. And they work with professional and student athletes to utilize their leadership roles and their unifying ability to heal what is in many ways a divided nation right now.

Through RISE, student athletes, these future professional athletes, are learning how to be not only effective athletes but also leaders in their field. The group's ten-week curriculum for high school and college student athletes teaches them about things like implicit bias and other ways in which race plays a role in our society, with an eye toward building leadership skills that can translate into being leaders on issues of equality and improving race relations.

RISE also collaborates with professional athletes who are already engaged with activism to empower them, provide information, connect them with others and with social justice organizations, and also help connect their activism to tangible change. For example, if there is an athlete who is interested in what is happening in Flint, Michigan, perhaps because he is from there or he has played in the Detroit market, RISE connects him or her with foundations they can be involved in so they can take their concerns and apply them in a way that is productive and effective.

In 2016, I spoke with Andrew MacIntosh, the national director of the leadership and education programs at RISE who helped create the group's curriculum, to discuss its impetus, directives, and why it might be needed at this time in the country, and why RISE decided to focus on athletes.

"Overall, what we want to do with RISE is improve race relations. There are two main ways we try to do that. The first bucket of things or activities in which we are engaged is education. Leadership and education programming, and that's the side of things that I primarily work on. We work to develop curriculum and engage with a variety of stakeholders at the high school level, the collegiate level, as well as community organizations to get our curriculum and materials imparted to coaches, student athletes, and others.

"We train coaches to have those conversations with their student athletes. It is coaches who student athletes are already familiar with, and they are having conversations with their student athletes about identity, about trust, about implicit bias, about the history of race and sport, about using sport as a vehicle, about leadership, about influencing others.

"We understand that coaches already have such a great relationship with their athletes that they are probably in one of the best positions to have some of these difficult conversations. Obviously, conversations about race and race relations are particularly challenging, and they've been made I think even more challenging by the events that have taken place in the US over the last six months to the last year or so.

"At the high school level, at the collegiate level, it's primarily about developing content, developing curriculum, and engaging with student athletes and their coaches to have some of these discussions. We do some work with nonprofits and community organizations, but primarily our educational programming is geared toward high school and college. There have been some middle schools. And we have worked as well with some professional organizations, within the NFL, and the NBA for instance.

"The second bucket of things we do is focused more on athletes who have already taken action or taken steps to become more active and vocal within this social justice space, as I would describe it. We are trying to help them to have greater impact and amplify their voices. That's been done through a series of town halls that we've had with various partners, and also by engaging with these athletes one-on-one, through a series of focus groups that we have had and will continue to have with athletes. All are geared, again, toward finding out, what is it that you hope to achieve? How can we assist? Are there others who can assist you? How could we bring you together with people who are already doing work in this space?

"We hope to empower athletes, athlete activism, and athlete leadership. We work with mainly those who are in the professional space, although there are some collegiate athletes there, those who have already decided to use their voice, decided to use their platforms, and we try to find ways and strategies in which we can help them and even make recommendations."

Athletes have a greater reach, a bond, a platform, and a phenomenal ability to connect with hundreds of thousands of people instantaneously. I asked MacIntosh if RISE instructs or cautions athletes about utilizing this immediate access. This is important because there has been backlash that comes from taking a stand or making an act in the moment, as we've seen with Colin Kaepernick, and with the Tampa Bay Buccaneers receiver Mike Evans, who protested the election of Donald Trump during a game by not standing for the anthem. How do you prepare the younger athletes and talk to some of the more established athletes about how to prepare or to come back from what can be at times substantial repercussions? Do you prepare them beforehand for how they should best make a statement or action? And do you talk to them about recouping once they have done something that has incurred a pushback?

"For me it has to be twofold. Athletes have to be prepared in advance of taking a stand. And certainly I would expect athletes to be taking stands throughout their careers, maybe not around a topic that might be so divisive, or a topic that might be so contentious, but I expect them to be taking stands throughout their careers because athletes have traditionally been leaders. Within their communities, within their schools. And we have looked to athletes to lead. We expect athletes to lead.

"I think the preparation for leadership is a critical piece for young athletes coming up. It's one of the reasons why we have the RISE high school leadership program, and it is framed in terms of leadership development. Because we see the ability to have conversations and to live and exist in a diverse world as an act of leadership. On the other hand yes, we have to prepare them to take a stand, to believe in the things that they think are important, to better reflect and understand who they are and understand and celebrate their differences and similarities with others. That is certainly a critical piece. But we simultaneously need to prepare them for the pushback, as you put it. What happens when people resist, or don't agree with the stand that you're taking?

"One way that we prepare our student athletes is with education. If you are going to take a stand, do you have all the facts around the issue? Do you have a sense of the history around the issue? Do you know what has taken place before you? Do you know others who have acted or stood up or spoken out within that space, and what are the lessons to be drawn from their actions? One of the things that came out as we chatted with athletes and had discussions is that they definitely see a need to be more educated as they begin to engage with those issues, and specifically this issue about race and race relations. They want to know what has happened, they want to know why we are at the point we are at, and they want to know what the next steps are from a best-practices standpoint.

"Educating individuals before they make a stand is important, but so is simultaneously educating them on tactics. If you had to make a stand, what are some good ways to make that stand? What are strategic ways to make that stand? What are the most meaningful ways to make that stand? I think if athletes know that going in, they can be far more effective as well.

"The other part is building a network that can support athletes who are willing to do some of this work. We aim to provide athletes who want to make a statement, who are taking these stands, with adequate support. Mentors who can help guide them. Civil rights and organizational leaders who can help them amplify their work and translate some of their protest into actions, tangible next steps. Colin Kaepernick has done a pretty decent job of not only speaking out but also donating money, and having conversations with colleges, high schools, and other community groups. That's the work that should take place after the protest, after the acts of activism, that continues us moving toward a progressively better society.

"A network that allows athletes, that supports athletes in making their statement and stand, and helps them translate that into tangible, effective next steps, I think is also an important step. And that's what comes after they've spoken out. It is a better preparation to be educated beforehand, educated on strategies and the more effective ways of speaking out and taking action, but simultaneously be provided with some support, so that when you act, when you speak out, you can be protected from the pushback that might occur."

Have you, I asked MacIntosh, or how do you address or try to combat the societal ideology or notion of athletes as entertainers and not informed people who should have or who could have an educated opinion? This notion that you're an athlete, which does not necessarily mean that you can also have an educated opinion, has been in the sports world for decades. Have you had discussions about this? Because that was some of the fallout that Colin Kaepernick was dealing with, that he is "pampered" and should just "shut up and play." Why do we as a society have this belief that an athlete can be immensely talented in one area but not also have opinions that are informed?

"Yes, some of that has come up. To address it we try to prepare athletes by providing them with information, by ensuring that they have support when they want to make some of these statements. Firstly, as we see in the case of Colin Kaepernick, he'd had several conversations with Dr. Harry Edwards. So when he spoke he was speaking from a very informed position. I think if athletes have support that can provide them with the facts, provide them with the strategies, that's one step.

"RISE started officially after about 2015. We began work with the high schools around the same time, so the winter of 2015 we did a pilot program with three high schools, and we're currently doing a year-long pilot with seven high schools in Detroit, where we're based, but we're rapidly expanding. By the end of the year, we're going to be having programming with high schools in at least five states. We're already working with six colleges, and a number of grassroots and nonprofit organizations across the country. We're rapidly expanding, but we've been doing this only about a year and a half.

"I think our curriculum, the conversations we have with the students, these skills that we build, are things that should be in every classroom. They used to be a part of our society, and slowly for a number of reasons they've been eroded. Some of these things the curriculum addresses is critical thinking, empathy, trust building, influencing others, conflict resolution—those are tangible skills that people need to function effectively in every aspect of their life. Certainly we see that once people have these skills, they're able to have conversations about race and race relations, but they're also able to have conversations about other things. I would like to see these skills being taught across the country, and being mentored and modeled by athletes at all levels across the country.

"Steve Ross was born and raised in Detroit, so our pilot programs have taken place in Detroit, and Detroit has gone through a real lean time over the past maybe five, six years. There was an economic decline, and a huge bankruptcy. He visited the city around the same time, and wanted to find some way to give back. Socioeconomic factors affect minorities in a more significant way than other factors. He wanted to find a way that he could contribute and give back to Detroit as well, which is why the program launched there.

"Finally, he, like me and many others, believes in the power of sport, the power of sport to overcome. Athletes are leaders; we look to them. And also when we are on the field, if you're on a team, you don't see race, you don't see color, you don't see age, you don't consider people's background. You're able to look past those things and see a teammate, a comrade.

"That idea, that notion, that feeling that sport brings, is also something that Steve Ross hopes we can teach to others as we have these discussions about race and race relations. Can we look past the fact that we might come from different racial groups or ethnicities or countries or backgrounds, and see the similarities that we have? That we are human beings who want to love, who need compassion, who have a great potential if we put our minds together, and can work in productive ways?"

MORE THAN JUST A GAME

Sometimes the End Justifies the Means

Looking at the support Colin Kaepernick has received from the sports world, the leagues, and his fans, it is clear that many people agree with his protest. Most of the backlash he has faced has to do with how he is protesting. Meanwhile, others may not agree with his protest because he is an athlete, and as such he should stick to sports and entertaining his fans. There is a part of our society that will never accept that sports is more than just entertainment. For many fans, sports is a means of escape. They escape the routine of their daily life by going to a game, or watching sports on TV. They do not want to have socioeconomic or political discussions that affect them on a daily basis enter the sports arena.

We will never change everyone, but I believe we can educate society about the role that athletes have played and can play in implementing change. Then I think slowly the notion of sports solely as entertainment will change. However, change does not happen without discomfort. It is the discomfort of protest that makes it newsworthy. It is this discomfort that creates a discourse and enables people with differing points of view to come together to discuss it and hopefully create change, or at the very least shine a light on the issues we are passionate about, that we think are unjust. It is precisely this feeling of discomfort that made me certain I had to do something about my incident with the police. When I look at the incidents of police misconduct or of unarmed men being shot and killed by law enforcement, in only the last few years, it makes me uncomfortable.

Despite repeated, often videotaped instances of violence against black Americans by people sworn to protect them, it is disturbingly apparent that few outside the black community want to accept what seems unquestionable: African Americans are disproportionately targeted due to systematic and institutionalized biases within the government and the police force. These biases often cost black Americans their lives. Yet America still questions the necessity of the Black Lives Matter movement. Somehow America still ponders—despite incident after incident—why there is so much distrust and public outrage at the daily injustices that occur, disproportionally, to people of color.

The thirteen-month US Justice Department investigation into the Chicago Police Department, conducted in January 2017, pointed to "a police department with a legacy of corruption and abuse." The inquiry comes "as the department grapples with skyrocketing violence in Chicago, where murders are at a 20-year high, and a deep lack of trust among the city's residents." The 161-page investigation then laid out a list of unchecked aggressions: "an officer pointing a gun at teenagers on bicycles suspected of trespassing; officers using a Taser on an unarmed, naked 65-year-old woman with mental illness; officers purposely dropping off young gang members in rival territory." The report found that officers often used excessive force against minorities and that their actions were "practically condoned by supervisors, who rarely questioned their actions."[1]

This investigation is only the latest conducted by the Justice Department into the police departments of Chicago and Baltimore, which have been besieged by violence and tension between the police and the public. In August 2016, the *New York Times* described an earlier Justice Department report, which found that "the Baltimore Police Department for years has hounded black residents who make up most of the city's population, systematically stopping, searching and arresting them, often with little provocation or rationale." The article that followed laid out a list of mostly unarmed black men and women (such as Sandra Bland) who were killed by the police either on the street or died while they were in police custody.

According to the *Times*, "investigations examined a slew of potentially unconstitutional practices, including excessive force and discriminatory traffic stops within the Baltimore Police Department. Among them: Black residents account for roughly eighty-four percent of stops, though they represent just sixty-three percent of the city's population."

"In one telling anecdote from the report," the *Times* article continued, "a [Baltimore Police Department] shift commander provided officers with boilerplate language on how to write up trespassing arrest reports of people found near housing projects. The template contained an automatic description of the arrestee: 'A BLACK MALE.'"

Because of social media and our twenty-four-hour news cycle, we are all too familiar with many of the victims. Within the last three years there has been an alarming number of African Americans killed at the hands of law enforcement. Perhaps the most shocking is the one that started the Black Lives Matter movement: the chokehold death of Eric Garner in 2014 in Staten Island. Garner was approached by police for selling loose cigarettes. When he told police that he was tired of being harassed, the officers went to arrest him. While he was being restrained by four police officers, Garner repeated "I can't breathe" eleven times while lying facedown on the sidewalk until he lost consciousness. Garner died an hour later at the hospital. The incident was filmed, and the video shared around the world for weeks. The subsequent outrage incited public rallies and riots. By December 2014, there were at least fifty nationwide protests against police brutality. In July 2015, an out-of-court settlement was reached. The City of New York would pay $5.9 million to Garner's family.

In Baltimore in 2015, Freddie Gray was arrested for possessing what the police alleged was an illegal switchblade. While being taken to the police station, Gray was found with his neck broken, still handcuffed and shackled in the police van. Gray's death threw Baltimore into turmoil and incited large protests and the worst riots the city had seen in decades. Despite the public outcry, prosecutors dropped the remaining charges and all convictions against Baltimore police officers in Gray's death.

Philando Castile's death on July 6, 2016, is perhaps the most harrowing. Castile was fatally shot by a Minnesota police officer, after being pulled over in Falcon Heights. Castile was driving with his girlfriend, Diamond Reynolds. After being asked for his license and registration, Castile told the officer he was licensed to carry a weapon and had one in the car. The officer told him not to move. As Castile was putting his hands back up, the officer shot him four times.

During the incident, Reynolds streamed a live video on Facebook. It shows Castile bleeding and dying. Her four-year-old daughter was in the car during the encounter. This incident followed another police shooting incident that same week in Baton Rouge, Louisiana, involving another black man, Alton Sterling. Sterling was tackled by police officers outside a store for selling CDs. He was then shot seven times and killed as two cops held him down on the ground. His death was also recorded, and the video was shared around the world via social media. News of his death incited protests and deadly police ambushes in Dallas and Baton Rouge.

On September 16, 2016, in Tulsa, Oklahoma, Terence Crutcher was on his way home when his car stalled. The police arrived shortly after responding to a call about a vehicle blocking traffic. Crutcher is captured on video walking toward his disabled vehicle with his hands raised, while Officer Betty Jo Shelby follows with her gun drawn. Moments after Crutcher reaches his vehicle, Officer Shelby fires her gun and kills him. While Crutcher is seen walking toward his car with his hands up, an officer remarks "this looks like a bad guy," but Crutcher, who was unarmed, had not committed any crime, resisted in any way, or given any indication that the officers had anything to fear from him. Aside from the fact that he was a large black man. The incident was also recorded and posted worldwide on social media. The shooting led to riots in Tulsa.

The *Times* article states, "The Supreme Court has given police officers wide latitude in how they can use deadly force, which makes prosecuting them difficult, even in the killing of unarmed people. For the Justice Department to charge an officer with a federal crime, the bar is even higher. Prosecutors must show that the officer willfully violated someone's civil rights. State and federal investigators cleared the officer who killed twelve-year-old Tamir Rice in Cleveland. Rice was playing with a plastic BB gun in the park when he was shot and killed by police."

I can come up with no other explanation when I look at these incidents, and the ensuing "blistering" Justice Department reports, than they happen in part because of discriminatory practices and implicit bias (why else would officers react negatively to Crutcher on sight?), and also because of a lack of training and sensitivity on the part of police officers in certain communities.

Before all the video accounts of these tragic deaths, America was starting to think that discrimination had gone away, that it was no longer an issue. It is 2014, people thought, and we have a two-term black president. We are living in a "post-racial" America; these types of things do not happen anymore. Then video after video started surfacing of police shootings of African American men, many *literally* running away, yet still getting shot. The public outcry was that it is getting worse. But the reality is, it is not getting worse, it's getting taped and shared and publicized. Because of social media, these images are being reposted, and retweeted, and are reaching people worldwide in moments.

It is important to understand that racism never went away, nor racial profiling, nor unconstitutional practices that target specific demographics, like stop-and-frisk practices, mass incarceration of certain demographics, the use of excessive force by the police, and a lack of accountability. I don't think racism and discrimination will ever go away until we create change in several areas, and one of them is in police conduct. This is a cause I am passionate about, and I will speak up and advocate for more oversight, even if it makes America and the media uncomfortable.

A little discomfort is okay if we can start a conversation about additional police training and practices, or necessary protocols, departmental oversight, and checks and balances, to ensure accountability. If a little discomfort leads to improved relations and interactions between the police and the public, then being uncomfortable is worth it, because sometimes the end justifies the means.

I recently spoke with a police chief in Connecticut who also shared the belief that what happened to me in New York was grossly unfair and should never happen. He believed that communication is a big factor that can help change policing. Communication between the police officers and the community as well as communication between the officers on the scene and the person they have in custody. He was also shocked to find out that there was no report written and that the four other officers stood by Frascatore's statement of what happened until they reviewed the video evidence, after which their report of the incident changed. Despite this, the police

chief truly does not believe there is still a "blue wall of silence."
I want to share his optimism, but when it happens to you, your
optimism starts to fade. I do share his view that open communication between the officers and the people in the communities they patrol is a step in the right direction. Longer
training, along with sensitivity and implicit bias training, are
also integral parts of the solution.

Although there are few people in America who do not
know about Kaepernick's protest, he is not the first professional athlete to take a public stand during the anthem. Not
many people are familiar with the former Denver Nuggets
guard Mahmoud Abdul-Rauf, who in 1996 faced severe repercussions for praying during the national anthem. Considered one of the greatest free-throw shooters in the history of
the game, Abdul-Rauf lost millions of dollars in endorsement
deals, and his nine-year NBA career was thrown into turmoil
when he was caught on camera praying during the anthem.
This drew the ire of fans and the media.

Abdul-Rauf refused to acknowledge the flag because it
conflicted with some of his Islamic beliefs. At first no one noticed, because he either stretched or stayed in the locker room
during the anthem, until a reporter asked him about it and his
response caused a media frenzy. Abdul-Rauf said he viewed
the American flag as "a symbol of oppression and racism," and
that standing for the anthem would conflict with his Muslim
faith. "You can't be for God and for oppression. It's clear in
the Quran, Islam is the only way," he said at the time. "I don't
criticize those who stand, so don't criticize me for sitting."

The NBA suspended him for one game, citing a rule that
players must line up in a "dignified posture" for the anthem.

"It cost him almost $32,000 of his $2.6 million salary," the journalist Jesse Washington wrote in the blog *The Undefeated*.

The players union supported Abdul-Rauf, and he quickly reached a compromise with the league that allowed him to stand and pray with his head down during the anthem. But at the end of the season, the Nuggets traded Abdul-Rauf, who averaged a team-high 19.2 points and 6.8 assists, to the Sacramento Kings. His playing time dropped. He lost his starting spot. After his contract expired in 1998, Abdul-Rauf couldn't get so much as a tryout with any NBA team. He was just 29 years old. . . .

After the NBA shunned him, he played a season in Turkey, making about half of the $3.3 million he earned in the last year of his NBA contract. Abdul-Rauf caught on with the NBA's Vancouver Grizzlies in 2000–2001, but played only 12 minutes per game. He never got another NBA opportunity, playing another six seasons in Russia, Italy, Greece, Saudi Arabia and Japan before retiring in 2011.[2]

Not only was Abdul-Rauf's career in jeopardy, but he and his family also received death threats. The letters "KKK" were spray painted on a sign near where his new home was being built. Abdul-Rauf decided to put the property up for sale, but while it sat vacant, it was set on fire and burned to the ground. He eventually moved his family to Europe, not only for their safety but also to be able to play professional basketball.

"It's priceless to know that I can go to sleep knowing that I stood to my principles," Abdul-Rauf told *The Undefeated*.

"Whether I go broke, whether they take my life, whatever it is, I stood on principles. To me, that is worth more than wealth and fame."

Abdul-Rauf has not spoken to Kaepernick. But the basketball player supports the quarterback's protest and message "1,000 percent," saying that it created a valuable debate. "It's good to continue to draw people's attention to what's going on whether you're an athlete, a politician, or a garbage man. These discussions are necessary," he said. "Sometimes it takes people of that stature, athletes and entertainers, because the youth are drawn to them, [more than] teachers and professors, unfortunately."[3]

Abdul-Rauf lost prime years of NBA stardom, faced severe financial fallout, received death threats against him and his family, had his home burned down, and had to leave the country to play professionally. Yet Abdul-Rauf still does not stand for the national anthem. In the 1990s, few athletes made public protests about social issues. Abdul-Rauf's protest was a pivotal moment that completely changed the course of his athletic career, and his life. He was a precursor to athletes like Kaepernick, and today's resurgence of athlete activists, who are inciting change and taking a stand against what they feel is unjust. As Abdul-Rauf said of the growing movement, "It is beautiful to see, and it's going to be hard to stop."

Postracial America?

When we look at discrimination sixty years ago during the years of integration, we can see that it was accepted, or at the very least it was expected. One of the major challenges then was being openly hated and harassed. Today, for the most part, hatred and harassment are much more behind the scenes. Social media has given people an anonymous voice and a platform from which they are free to speak their mind. Because of this shift, the challenge that athletes who advocate for a cause face is to have to read about, and see, the often vitriolic responses. They are faced day after day, even minute by minute, in the continuous news cycle and on social media, with insults, disparaging comments, and sometimes even threats. We can never know how real those threats are, as opposed to back when they were very real. Abdul-Rauf left the country not only to play professional basketball but also because he feared for his safety and that of his family.

If one of those threats turned physical, there were no social media or video accounts to shed light on what really happened or to prove one person's word over another. Players were also more isolated and perhaps even more insulated. Sixty years ago, racism was the norm. The Klan was a very real danger and part of everyday life in many parts of the country. Jim Crow laws were still in effect and there were still many people who spoke openly and publicly about segregation. In many parts of the country it was widely accepted that there were genetic differences between blacks and whites and that blacks were inferior. This kind of thinking now seems absurd, but especially considering it was common only sixty years ago, you have to wonder if it ever went away. The considerations of protesting in the South were very different from protesting in the North. In the South, civil rights activists would face openly hostile disagreement and also perhaps deadly repercussions.

These deadly repercussions, or any actions against you,

could even be justified in court and the justice system at that time. There was an overriding feeling that blacks had no right to protest anything. Those days, it was not just your money, or your endorsements, sponsors, or your fan base at stake; it could also be your life. There was the possibility that you could be lynched by the Klan, that your home could be burned down, your property destroyed, or even that your family could be in jeopardy. Just twenty years ago, Abdul-Rauf encountered that type of aggression.

Those are some of the dangers you faced in the past if you were advocating for racial equality or against discrimination. The plus side was that it was before social media and you could shut it out. You could far more easily disconnect from the news and not have to be aware of the media all the time. Today it is very difficult to get away from the news. It is far too easy to check in with Twitter, or Facebook, or turn on the news, which is available 24/7. Our smartphones are continuously updating us with alerts. In some cases, this easy access to information can be useful, but in others, it can be unrelenting.

For a while back in September, October, and November 2016 it was definitely unrelenting. It seemed like every day there was a new case of an unarmed person of color being shot and killed by the police. Quite often these people weren't doing anything illegal, like Philando Castile, or Terence Crutcher. This type of constant media information will either empower us to rally together in protest using social media and all the news outlets at our disposal, or it will immobilize us, shock us into catatonia, as we disconnect to get away from it.

I am astonished that so many Americans think that because we had a two-term black president, racism no longer exists. Even when it is right in front of them, as with the many videotaped shootings of black men, they still do not believe it. The general response is that the victims had to have done something wrong. This speaks directly to my incident. I was standing in the middle of the street minding my own business when I was tackled by a police officer for something I was completely innocent of.

It is a sad commentary, because we don't want to believe the statistics. According to a 2015 *Los Angeles Daily News* article, "American police kill civilians at a shocking rate compared to other developed countries. . . . While no US government agency is keeping reliable records of how many people die each year during encounters with police, the best estimates suggest the number is no lower than 400 per year, and most likely around 1,000. Police in peer nations like Germany, Denmark, the UK and other liberal democracies—meanwhile—rarely kill civilians. Even accounting for population size, the frequency with which American police kill civilians is shocking. Not twice as often, or three times as often. We're talking factors of 20 to 70."

The *Washington Post*'s police shootings database reports that 991 people were killed by police in 2015, and 963 people were shot and killed by police in 2016, "many of whom were unarmed, mentally ill, and people of color." That number is much higher, according to the *Guardian*'s police killings database, Killed by Police, which counts 1,092 people to have died at the hands of police in 2016. Going by the *Guardian*'s count, Native Americans and black Americans are being killed at the highest rates in the United States. February and March were the deadliest months in 2016, with 100 people killed by police each *month*.

Michelle Alexander, a law professor at Ohio State, wrote in her bestseller, *The New Jim Crow: Mass Incarceration in the Age of Colorblindness*, that in 2012, when the book was published, "more Black men are in prison or jail, on probation or parole than were enslaved in 1850, before the Civil War began." If these statistics do not seem like an inequity in America I think we should ask ourselves why not. America does not want to believe in prison for profit or the mass incarceration of African Americans. We do not want to believe in police brutality or misconduct unless we see it. Then, when we do see videos of it, we still do not want to believe it. Why do we think these incidents have nothing to do with race or discrimination? It is baffling that so many people do not believe that racism still exists when in the last few years there has been a surge in racial violence and instances of police misconduct against minorities.

In today's "postracial" America there are still practices, like stop and frisk, that are targeted to certain segments of the population. Or stand-your-ground laws, which seem biased toward one part of the population, if we consider the 2012 shooting death of seventeen-year-old Trayvon Martin in Florida. Meanwhile this same law protects others, like George Zimmerman, who shot and killed Martin. It seems inherently dangerous for the use of deadly force to be condoned because someone *feels* like they are in danger and can shoot to kill even if the person they have shot *does not actually* pose a threat.

Open-carry laws also seem more partial to one segment of the population while at times being a death sentence for others, like Philando Castile. This law protects armed militia groups like the Ammon Bundy ranchers in Oregon, who took over government land in January and February in 2016, and *literally* threatened the police with an arsenal of weapons unless their demands were met. The militia will serve no prison time. Meanwhile in Cleveland, Ohio, Tamir Rice, a twelve-year-old black boy playing in a park with a BB gun, was immediately shot and killed by police. This case in particular is made all the more confounding because Ohio is an open-carry state. If the gun was a real gun and not a plastic one, Rice would not have been breaking a law to have it, and his having it should not have warranted such a police response.

Today, with President Trump making it okay to advance racist ideology, by condemning an entire religion for the acts of minority extremists, I do not see policy becoming more fair toward minorities. Rather, I see the opposite. Even the phrase that won Trump the election, "Make America Great Again," appears to want to invoke a time in America that was never "great" for minorities. It reads like a claim to take America back to the days of Jim Crow segregation and open discrimination, some of which we have already seen postelection with hate crimes against minorities and Muslims. "Make America Great Again" sounds like a rally cry to go back to the days when it was okay to be openly racist and discriminatory, as with his Muslim bans, proposed walls separating America from Mexico, xenophobia, rolling back women's rights, voter disenfranchisement, and voter suppression. It is a slippery slope to be hostile and inflammatory to a segment of the population or want to punish an entire religion, and it should remind America of the dark days of its past.

Societal Expectations
of Sports Stars

When athletes take a stand, we can jeopardize our earning potential and our financial security. It can be detrimental financially, societally, emotionally, and even physically to advocate for a cause or to publicly voice our opinion. Certainly for Abdul-Rauf and Kaepernick there have been repercussions. They have gotten vicious vocal backlash from the media, and have affected their careers and their ability to play in terms of endorsements and marketing dollars. These selfless acts are reason enough to be impressed by athlete activists who are gambling far more than fan appeal. These are considerations every professional athlete who decides to speak out for a cause takes into account.

It is one thing to take a stand, but for Kaepernick to donate a million dollars of his own money or to donate the money that he's made from his jersey sales to community organizations is another. This tells me that he is willing to make sacrifices for what he believes in. It also tells me that his protest is not only a symbolic gesture but also a very tangible act.

More so than just a personal backlash, Kaepernick is also making monetary sacrifices at the same time. People may say, "Well, he makes twelve million dollars, so how does donating one million dollars really affect him?" But what the public does not realize is that an athlete's career, depending on the sport, tends to be short. In the NFL the average career is three years. Right now, Kaepernick is already playing on borrowed time.

Professional athletes retire a lot earlier than age sixty-five.

A football player still going hard at forty is rare. Most athletes either retire or leave the game in their thirties. I retired from playing professional tennis at thirty-three. When we retire so early in our career, we need enough money to take care of our family. Sadly, it has become common to vilify the athlete as pampered. Fans read about big salaries and think we should just be grateful for our salaries for playing a game, and that part of our job is to entertain them and not to have an opinion while doing it. Many of these fans also believe they have a right to this opinion because they pay our salary by buying tickets to our games, or merchandise.

But athletes' ability to make a considerable amount of money in contracts or endorsements is not a reason for fans, the media, or even our franchises or sponsors to think it allows them to have control over what we think, do, or feel passionate about. Why should athletes, because we make a certain amount of money, not feel we can express our opinion and concentrate only on sports?

Why are we criticized for feeling strongly about an issue and wanting to do something about it? Why can't we question what is going on in the world or want to see change? That is what I am doing when I speak out publicly about more accountability and oversight for law enforcement. This is what LeBron James, Dwayne Wade, and several of their Miami Heat teammates were doing when they wore hoodies before a game to protest the killing of Trayvon Martin and police brutality. That is what Chris Kluwe, Scott Fujita, and Brendon Ayanbadejo are doing when they lobby for LGBT rights and marriage equality. That is what Venus Williams, Maria Sharapova, and Kim Clijsters are doing when they rally for equal prize money for female tennis players, and what Serena Williams is doing when she speaks out for equal endorsement deals and equal recognition for female tennis players.

This is what Mahmoud Abdul-Rauf did when he was true to his beliefs, even to the detriment of his career and even if it placed him in harm's way. This is what Colin Kaepernick is doing when he takes a knee during the national anthem to support Black Lives Matter. Sadly, what is lost in all the media outrage, and what we should understand, is that what Kaepernick is doing is not denigrating or disrespecting the flag or the country. He is exercising his inalienable right to respond to the anthem in a way that feels genuine and authentic to him. That distinction has also been lost.

What activist athletes are saying is, Why can't this be better? How can we draw attention to issues that are important to us, that we are passionate about? Why should we not be able to express our position on it? Why are we not allowed to have an opinion outside sports? Where did the notion that we are only there to entertain the fans come from? The idea that we are not allowed to publicly voice our opinion because of how much money we make is oppressive, and undercuts our rights as Americans. Ultimately, the amount of money someone makes should not disqualify him or her from having an opinion and expressing it, especially if it can create a positive change.

Just like anyone else in America, athletes should be able to have an opinion and to act on it. In so many ways, that is what being an American citizen and living in this country is about. These freedoms are what America was built on and what we as a country and a nation fought so hard for. When being a professional athlete brings with it stipulations about how we can voice our opinions, or *if* we can even have an opinion because of preconceived notions of what we can contribute to the social discourse, it is akin to having our First Amendment right to freedom of speech taken away, or at the very least, muffled.

Yet when we look at the contributions of so many athletes over the last several decades, whether in sports, through philanthropy, or through social change, it is clear that those contributions cannot be denied or downplayed. Over the last seventy years, athletes have changed social, political, and educational policy. We have started a social discourse on women's rights, marriage equality, and LGBT rights, and have made strides in each of those areas. As seen throughout history, through some of the phenomenal athlete activists profiled in *Ways of Grace*, when we advocate to create change and use our global platform, network, and resources, the world notices, and things *do* change.

This ability to create change is one of the reasons why it is such a promising sign that Kaepernick's protest has gotten so much media attention. Regardless of if it is positive or negative, the media is drawing attention to it. However, some of the most confounding criticisms I have heard about Kaepernick from pundits and the public is that police brutality is not the most detrimental thing happening in the African American community. Whether that is true or not, Black Lives Matter is a cause that is important to him. He should not have to concern himself with issues that people think are more important. His causes should be his own. I would not want to be told to focus on issues other than the ones I want to talk about, write about, research, or advocate about.

My sport, tennis, is an individual-player sport, in which

you worry about your own career, and you don't have to answer to a league, franchise, or a team. I don't know personally the repercussions or ramifications of protesting as a team player. I can't imagine how it must feel to kneel during the anthem while your teammates stand around you. I do not have to be in sync with the team, I am out there alone. Taking a stand as a team-sport player comes with many more considerations because you are also drawing attention to your team, your teammates, and your league. This makes what Kaepernick and his supporters in the NBA, the NFL, and the WNBA are doing all the more brave and admirable.

I have talked to a few football players who say that playing in a divided locker room is detrimental to the team's success. No matter how much talent you have, not playing as a unified team will undercut the efficiency of the players, the morale, and their play as a team. It will show on the field. When you consider that Kaepernick had to know this going in, you have to commend his commitment. We, as athletes and as people, do not do something that can negatively affect us unless we strongly believe in what we are doing. But what I have heard from people closely associated with the 49ers is that they are not divided. Kaepernick's team and the organization are behind him, and believe in what he is doing. Or, they have not spoken out against it.

Activism is never easy. Speaking up in any way about anything, especially when you are in the public eye, is even harder, because public figures are easy targets. To be told or made to feel that what we are passionate about is not what we should be passionate about stifles our expression and robs us of our freedoms and civil liberties.

A PERSONAL CHOICE

The Athlete as Activist

In generations past, for athletes to make a statement, to make audiences stand up and take notice, it took monumental firsts, like when Jackie Robinson integrated Major League Baseball in 1947, or when Arthur Ashe became the first African American man to win at Wimbledon and the US Open, and to be ranked number one in the world. Now any professional athlete with a Twitter account can let the world know how he or she feels. The issues we face in America now, at first glance, may not seem as important as those in the civil rights era, but to activists today, the realization is that we are still fighting the same battles—racism, inequality, discrimination, sexism, voting rights—and that fact is disheartening. It may be even more of an uphill battle, because so many people today want to deny that these issues still exist.

Athlete activists are actually speaking up more than they did in the past, even though the stakes are much higher financially. The instant access of social media and the amount of attention given to athletes makes it easier for us to have a voice. So many of us are able to turn a gesture into a statement. And as we have seen, even a small act can make big waves.

Right now, in our society, divisiveness is at an all-time high. The civil rights and civil liberties that activists fought for in the past seem so clear-cut today. I wonder if thirty years from now, this will be the case with the issues we are speaking up about, like voting rights, voter ID laws, marriage equality, equal access to bathrooms for transgender people, or the Black Lives Matter movement. There are not many people today who would openly suggest that Jackie Robinson's integrating baseball was not the right thing to do, but there is a debate about the racial and equality issues we face today. It is important for the athlete to have these types of public discussions today. Our platform and unprecedented fan and media access allows this new generation of athlete activists to use their voices exponentially.

Though not everyone is an activist, everyone can lead. Everyone can make a difference or make a statement, but not everyone is an activist. Activism is isolating. Activism is polarizing. To any athlete considering becoming more involved in or aligning with a cause you are passionate about, I would say this: Truly consider what you are fighting for and why. Form your opinion and talk to people in your camp whom you trust, and to your family. Be informed about what you are advocating for. Then consider the best way to convey your message before you go public. Then consider carefully *how* to go public. It could be during a press conference, a social media protest, or in a statement on your uniform or wardrobe. However you choose to make your statement, be ready for the consequences of your actions, whatever they might be.

I would caution you that becoming active during your career will take time and energy away from the sport you are committed to. I was so singularly focused on tennis during my twenties that it would have been much harder for me to take the time away for any advocacy. If I were constantly second-guessing myself for not doing enough, it would have negatively affected my career. This is a personal and individual choice. I am proud of the athletes who make the decision to be activists during their active careers. Your sacrifice is twofold: not only are you leaving yourself open to public criticism and rebuke, your activism can also take away from your professional career. Keep in mind that advocacy, if you are fully committed, will draw attention away from the sport and divide your attention, which could make your game suffer.

I also want to caution you to be prepared to lose people you may have considered your friends. You should expect that not everyone will want you to speak out about what you feel is unjust or about an area that could be strengthened in our society. Understand that it will make some people uncomfortable; change is always uncomfortable. That is something you will have to take into consideration before taking a stand—if you are willing and able to stand firm under pressure from the media, the public, your teammates, your league, and even your friends. It takes a certain mind-set and mentality to be able to handle that. Jackie Robinson may not have been the best player ever in the Negro Leagues, but he was widely regarded, because of his patience, focus, and drive, as the player who was best prepared to handle the inevitable backlash when he stepped on the baseball field with the Dodgers.

If you are not prepared, the media attention and potential backlash will overwhelm you. Your already public life will become even more public, and your private life will be put under a microscope. This was the case with the Tampa Bay Buccaneers receiver Mike Evans. In November 2016 he protested the election of Donald Trump during a Salute to Service Day game against the Chicago Bears by not standing for the anthem. When he received substantial backlash, he backed off and issued an apology a few days later. A part of his apology read, "I know I've hurt a lot of people by doing what I did. I'm sorry to those who are truly affected by what I did, to those who are disappointed in what I did, and to my teammates."

I assume Evans was not apologizing for his belief, but for the way he made his statement. If that is the case, although well intended, he seems not to have accomplished either. By not fully committing to his stand, he disappointed his supporters, who may have felt he did not fully represent them. At the same time, he also angered his fans with his gesture. His apology has gotten more media attention than his act, and that is the last impression his fans will have. Although he tried to further a good cause, he has gotten backlash from all sides for a gesture that could be seen as courageous.

Most important: Be prepared. Do your homework before you do anything publicly. Consider all the repercussions of your actions, to your family, your teammates, and your franchise. Read and research what is happening in the media with other athlete activists, especially those who are supporting the same cause. Talk to your coach, your agent, your teammates, your family, or other athlete activists. Get their feedback to make an informed decision. This preparedness is not to decide *if* you should take a stand—you have a right to back any cause you feel passionate about—but *how* you should go about it. Only when you have taken all this into consideration, then, and only then, should you go public with your protest or opinion.

Keep in mind though, an action is not activism. If advocacy is not ongoing, it may not have the momentum it needs to, as Billie Jean King said, change hearts and minds. For activism and advocacy to create change, you must continue to make a statement, to ask hard questions, and to draw attention to important societal issues, regardless of how unpopular it might make you, or how uncomfortable it might make your fans or the media.

It is important that we use the full extent of our resources and network to further our message, in big and small ways. When we look at Billie Jean King's forty-year career, we see that her activism spans almost the length of it. She has been a tireless activist since she started playing tennis in the sixties. King founded the Women's Tennis Association and advocated for the passage of Title IX, which allowed female athletes access to sports scholarships. King has fought for women's rights and representation in sports, for gay rights, and for marriage equality for decades. With her Leadership Initiative, she is now fighting to promote diversity and inclusion in the workplace. And King does not always advocate in a very public way. Her work is often in the background, but it has been ongoing for the last four decades.

It is also just as important to believe in what you choose

to advocate for. That might seem like odd advice, but you will not be able to face opposition without an unwavering conviction and belief in what you stand for. I truly believe that we need changes in how some police officers conduct themselves on the job. I want to speak up for anyone who has faced misconduct, but does not have the media access or resources to make his or her voice heard. I will always be passionate about this cause. But I accept that many people have a different view. It is hard to understand how someone else feels unless you have walked a mile in his or her shoes. But I would never wish what I went through on anyone else. This is the reason why I will continue fighting to make sure there are procedures, protocols, and oversight, and any necessary training, to stop what happened to me from happening to anyone ever again. And if it does happen, that there is accountability.

"We Don't Choose to Be Role Models, We Are Chosen"

Athletes have a voice and a platform that so many others do not have, because we have fans. Our fans love and support us. They appreciate the dedication it took for us to have risen up through the ranks. Our fans look up to us for the hard work we put in to get to the highest level of accomplishment in a sport. They appreciate that we give back to them when we play hard, that we entertain them and make them proud to cheer us on.

Our fans may relate to us because a game got them through a tough time, or created more of a bond with a friend, spouse, or family member as they sat and watched their favorite athlete or team week after week. The type of bond between the athlete and their fans is powerful and unique to the sports world. Because of this, we have the ability to speak to and influence millions of people, with a gesture before a game, in a tweet, a post, or a picture on Instagram, or in a comment during a press conference. This type of platform is not something to be taken lightly, and when it is, we have seen the consequences. But when we first consider the ramifications of our actions, when we arm ourselves with knowledge and foresight, and if we are passionate about and committed to our cause, we *can* change policy. We can do good, we can incite change, and we can change lives. I know this because athlete activists like Billie Jean King, Arthur Ashe, Tommie Smith, John Carlos, Colin Kaepernick, Brendon Ayanbadejo, Chris Kluwe, Amir Hadad, Aisam-Ul-Haq Qureshi, Venus and Serena Williams, and so many others have already done it.

Charles Barkley said in his controversial 1993 Nike commercial, "I am not a role model." He was arguing that being a professional athlete does not make him a de facto role model. But when more teenagers aspire to be professional athletes than to be the president, we can't deny that what athletes do affects the next generation. I agree with the response of the basketball superstar Karl Malone to Barkley in a *Sports Illustrated* column: "Charles . . . I don't think it's your decision to make. We don't choose to be role models, we are chosen. Our only choice is whether to be a good role model or a bad one."

As professional athletes, we can't control whether or not we are role models. What we can control is if we want to use our influence and platform in a positive or negative way. We *are* role models whether we want to be or not. Young people pay attention to what we do. If they see us doing positive things outside our sport, like trying to create positive change through advocacy or activism, they will take notice and they may be inspired to do the same. But making a statement is not something we can ever take lightly. We have a fundamental right as Americans to voice our opinion, but as professional athletes constantly in the public eye, we must remember that it is up to us to make the right choices about how we deliver our message, because it affects not only this generation, but the next. Up-and-coming athlete activists like Nigel Hayes, Jordan Hill, and Bronson Koenig of the University of Wisconsin basketball team are watching us. Young men who aspire to be the best in their sport and play professionally are watching us. Our fans are watching us. Our teammates, our league, the media, are definitely watching us. Let's use our visibility, media access, and voice to make the world a more positive, inclusive place for everyone.

Change Makes People Uncomfortable

"Start where you are. Use what you have. Do what you can." Arthur Ashe's words inspired me to use my situation to help those who don't have the platform or the access to the media that I have. My impetus to speak out was based on a very personal incident, but such a catalyst does not always have to be something that is so personal or personally connected to you. It seems like today there is not as much outrage over what is happening in the world. When someone like Donald Trump, our newly elected president, calls for a ban on Muslims and their religion or says something inflammatory or outright xenophobic, people who don't know Muslims or aren't friends with Muslims do not react because it does not affect them *personally*. But when Trump made derogatory comments about women there was justifiable outrage, because every man has a woman in his life: his wife, mother, sister, friend, or a girlfriend. This is the source of the outrage, not because what he is saying or doing is intrinsically wrong.

We do not need a personal connection to feel outrage, but often that is the case. There are many examples of public servants who have changed their stance on policy after it affected a member of their family. For instance, Dick Cheney changed his stance on LGBT rights after his daughter came out. It can be difficult to realize the full impact that some policies have until they affect a loved one. I do not believe many people feel outraged to see so many videotaped deaths of innocent unarmed black men, because it may not hit close to home. Many of these incidents also die down quickly, as the media continuously replenishes itself. Keeping them prominent in the media is part of the greater purpose of activist athletes.

We should feel outrage any time someone is being persecuted or treated unfairly. Even if you come from a community where you do not see police misconduct or discrimination because there are not a lot of African Americans or Latinos in your neighborhood it does not mean that it is not happening, or that you should not feel outrage or want to do something about it. Investigate the incidents. Do some research. Dig a little deeper to see why Colin Kaepernick is supporting Black Lives Matter, or why Chris Kluwe, Brendon Ayanbadejo, and Scott Fujita are advocating for marriage equality. Look up

Athlete Ally and see how Hudson Taylor and the athletes who are members are fighting for LGBT rights.

Change is never easy and does not happen without discomfort. Talking about my incident in the media is not comfortable. Writing about it is not comfortable. It was embarrassing to see myself on the ground in the video with Officer Frascatore's knee in my back. It was frustrating to feel helpless as I pleaded with the officers to uncuff me and to look at my ID to prove my identity. It was incredibly humbling to have absolutely no control over a situation that I was completely innocent of. It was and still is hard to think about and to recount it over and over again. But it is precisely that feeling of discomfort that made me certain that I had to do something about it.

That is why it is important for me to draw attention to police misconduct and the lack of accountability for unconstitutional practices that target specific demographics, like stop-and-frisk practices, mass incarceration, misconduct, and the use of excessive force by police officers. If not, there will never be change. And in today's climate, with the riots in Tulsa and Baltimore and the deadly police ambushes in Dallas and Baton Rouge, our officers will continue to stay at risk. These issues will not go away until we create change. This is a cause I am passionate about and will speak up about, even if it makes America and the media uncomfortable.

A little discomfort is okay if we are furthering a message that can not only save lives but also heal some of the discord between law enforcement and our communities. If we can start a conversation about extending police training with additional psychological testing, or instituting necessary protocols and checks and balances, and even advocating for an overhaul of the system to ensure accountability, then being uncomfortable is a small price to pay, because sometimes the end justifies the means.

My journey from September 9, 2015, has left me saddened and angry still. It lessens at times, but then the flames of anger are often fanned when I see other incidents of misconduct. Or they are fanned when I wake up at night and think about how differently things could have turned out if I had been more reactive or tried to defend myself. Or if my wife and young children or any of my family had been there to see what happened, or had tried to protect me. Or had it not been noon in the middle of a city with hundreds of witnesses present, would this officer, with a history of using excessive force, have felt a license to do whatever he wanted, especially with four other officers to corroborate his story?

It makes me angry when I think about the lack of accountability for Officer Frascatore, who showed no remorse and did not even seem concerned about what had happened. He was not stripped of his job. I have to assume, after reviewing public record and speaking to other officers, that with the yearly automatic pay increases with years of service, Frascatore received a raise the year following the incident. To me, that does not seem like a deterrent and leads me to believe that my incident, which was not his first, will also not be his last. Officers who show a pattern of misconduct—whether they are because of personality issues, training issues, discrimination issues, or a lack of respect for the public—should be held accountable, so it does not happen again. When I consider this, and the Justice Department reports of the excessive force and misconduct by the Baltimore and Chicago Police Departments, or the alarming statistics of how many unarmed people are killed by officers, it becomes even clearer that some level of account-ability in law enforcement is vital, not only for the public but also to protect our police officers.

Sadly, my passion has been misconstrued by some fans and critics as being antipolice. This could not be further from the truth, as I remain proud of my grandfather's service as a New York police officer. But this is also why I was so confused and upset at my treatment by Officer Frascatore. I know accidents happen. Quite often our police officers have seconds to make life-and-death decisions. I can't imagine how stressful their jobs must be. Frascatore made a mistake. But to be so cavalier and unrepentant, to not even say sorry, after such an aggressive physical assault, was troubling and deeply unsettling. Then to find out that the five police officers stood together and cor-roborated each other's story until the video evidence surfaced and they reviewed it, confirmed to me that there is something deeply wrong with the system.

I respect our police, but the next time an officer approaches me, I am not sure I will trust him. This distrust hinges not only on the incident but because the officers who were on the scene stood together and denied what actually happened. If not for the video, it would have been my word against theirs. This made me wonder how often situations like this happen. As someone who has played professional tennis for over a de-cade, against some of the top players in the world, I like to think that I am pretty calm and cool under pressure, but I was flustered. I didn't get their badge numbers, their names, or even their precinct. I was too stunned by what had happened. When I was told, "Okay, you're free to go," I walked away in a daze instead of getting pertinent information to be able to follow up with their superiors. And the officers went about their business as though it did not affect them at all.

It is these officers who are giving the police force a bad name. That is not fair to the cops who are doing a good job and making the right decisions in the moment. It is unfair to law enforcement officers who do not have a history of discriminatory practices, who have the training they need to be sensitive and impartial and fair. I want to use my voice to speak out to help raise awareness and accountability and make sure that any officer with a discriminatory pattern of behavior gets the training he or she needs. These changes would make the police force stronger overall. It would also help restore the trust that the public should have in the police officers in their city and in their neighborhoods. It could reduce misunderstandings between the police and the public, which would ultimately save lives.

Perhaps with longer police training we would have fewer incidents like the ones that claimed the lives of Terence Crutcher, Walter Scott, Philando Castile, Alton Sterling, Eric Garner, Freddie Gray, Tamir Rice, Sandra Bland, Michael Brown . . . The length of time required to complete police academy training averaged nineteen weeks as of 2006, according to the Bureau of Justice Statistics. The Memphis Police Department Academy usually takes twenty-one weeks to complete, while San Diego's program lasts six months. Instead of six months of police training, maybe it should be a year, or sixteen months, or two years. Training our police officers is not an area where we can be too cautious.

Our officers have taken an oath to protect and to serve.

When they walk out onto the street to do their job, there is always the possibility they may have to use deadly force. When someone is given this type of responsibility, there is no such thing as too much training, too much readiness, too much sensitivity, too much knowledge, too many rules of conduct, or too much foresight. Our police officers are in the line of fire. It is only fair to thoroughly prepare them for anything they might encounter. To think that trainees can go through police academy training in six months, it seems a bit too soon to have the power to make life-or-death decisions. I don't know anyone who would feel comfortable going to a doctor who had only six months of training. I certainly would not.

Ultimately, we all want the same thing: Americans want to feel safe around law enforcement. Police officers, I would imagine, want to feel respected and trusted by the people they have sworn to protect and to serve. To that end, I support anything that strengthens and protects the police and the public. It will not only strengthen the bonds between the police and the public, but also make them both safer. It is imperative that at this time in our history we build up the trust between the public and the police in the areas where it is sorely lacking.

I have lost a few friends since I started talking about my incident in the media. They do not like that I have spoken out on behalf of my race, or my rights, or that I'm making public the officers' inappropriate conduct, or speaking out in any way against law enforcement. I cannot imagine that if they were true friends, that my advocating for a cause that is so personal and important to me, to give voice to my beliefs—beliefs that have been shaped by the events in my life—would jeopardize our friendship. I also cannot imagine that my right to voice my opinion to create positive change would seem unnecessary or inflammatory to them. So perhaps I have not lost any real friends. I am blessed to still have so many people in my life with whom I can disagree about political, racial, economic, or social issues, have productive discussions about them, and at the end of the day acknowledge that each of us has the right to those opinions.

Although I have lost some friends, I have gained new friends and supporters. The athletes who took time out of their busy schedules to speak to me and to share their journey, experiences, and perspective lifted me up more than they know. Their insight has been illuminating, enlightening, and empowering. This became especially true when I found out that although there was something each of them might have done differently, not one of them said they would *not* have taken a stand.

In 2013 I retired from professional tennis, and in 2015 I became the chairman of the USTA Foundation, which is the charitable arm of the association. Its mission is to change the lives of youth through tennis and educational scholarships, as well as enable people with disabilities, injured service members, veterans, and their families to gain access to tennis facilities, equipment, and resources. To date, the foundation has awarded more than $19 million in grants and scholarships to more than 270 programs. My new role as chairman is incredibly fulfilling because it speaks directly to my childhood experiences.

I learned to play tennis at the Harlem Junior Tennis and Education Program (HJTEP) in New York. It is a volunteer-based program that allows kids to play tennis there if they maintain a B average in school, which they show by bringing in their report card. It also had a "homework club" where you could go to study and get help with your schoolwork if you were having any trouble. Those types of programs directly benefit from the work of the USTA Foundation, and HJTEP was extremely beneficial to me. It is because I had access to those resources that I want to give back and lend my name and time to raise funds to create more programs like it, and improve the existing ones around the country. The upgrades I have already seen are remarkable. There are some facilities that have computer labs. Access to technology is vitally important in today's digital age and can keep the kids who do not have computers at home from falling behind. Programs like HJTEP teach kids at a young age the importance of schoolwork and allow them to be competitive in education as well as in athletics.

In this way, tennis serves as a tool that helps children reach their full potential and benefits them, their family, their community, and society. Although it is really not the goal of the program, I know it helped me to become a professional tennis player. More important, it created many scholarship athletes, college graduates, and other successful attendees of the program. It also teaches from a very young age the importance of giving back. When I became the best tennis player at the program, I helped out kids in the homework club. As a child I realized how to be appreciative of the opportunities afforded to me and what I could do to help others have the same opportunities. These early experiences have informed me in my new position as chairman and have shown me how important a role they play, as well as opening my eyes to the foundations that help make them possible.

The lessons I learned at HJTEP from the volunteers there

(one of them being my father) have carried over into my life after tennis. I always felt that the events I did for charity were more important than the matches I played on the tour because they had a greater impact on a larger number of people. I have no idea how far my new role outside professional tennis will take me. It is similar to when I started my tennis career and could not even imagine what I could accomplish or the doors that would open because of it. In these new endeavors, I want to open doors and create opportunities for others. That would mean so much more to me than anything I have accomplished on the tennis court. Making a difference, giving back, and changing the lives of others is much more fulfilling and important than anything I could do for myself.

As I progress in my professional life and the new roles and responsibilities I take on, it is sometimes a struggle to balance activism and my career. There is a steep learning curve when there is no rule book for this whole activism thing. But then no activist, or anyone speaking out for a cause, ever had a rule book. What all such individuals have—historically and today—are the same qualities: heart, faith, strength, perseverance, patience, passion, and an unwavering commitment to a cause. If you have those qualities, you are well on your way.

It is my hope that athletes speaking out will not be the exception but the rule, which is part of the challenge that we have had. During the civil rights era, we had a number of athletes speaking out. Over the last months of 2016, athletes taking a stand about social justice has emerged again. We should continue and build on this momentum. We should also support and celebrate the athletes who have stepped up, and encourage others to do the same. And while race and race relations are certainly serious issues that should be addressed, athletes can be leaders in other causes as well: the environment, gender equality, marriage equality, religious freedoms—causes that will change and improve the wider society and the world. We, their teammates, the league, the fans, the media, society, should support them. We should engage in meaningful discourse with them to broaden their perspective and their stance. If we do, over time, more athletes will feel comfortable speaking up and they will also be better educated and informed on how to do so. But we have to keep the momentum moving forward.

I am not the same person I was two years ago, before the incident. My perception of the world was changed irrevocably that sunny September afternoon. Although at times I wish it had never happened, it has changed me in many ways for the better. I have been through a lot in my life and I have had many ups and downs. I was given a second chance at my tennis career after I broke my neck halfway through it. That monumental setback gave me the focus, drive, and determination to get better, but also the awareness that my career could end at any time and I should appreciate every day that I am able to do what I love.

My incident in 2015 opened my eyes and showed me that I could use my voice, and my platform, to incite positive change that could create a ripple effect. As Mahmoud Abdul-Rauf said about the growing movement, "It is beautiful to see, and it's going to be hard to stop." It is my hope that *Ways of Grace* can start a conversation and show not only how athletes are creating change, but that we can *all* make a difference.

The Power of Protest

The end of 2016 and the beginning of 2017 has been a time of racial, social, and political unrest in the United States. It was marked by strained race relations between law enforcement and the black community, and a unique presidential campaign charged with racial rhetoric and capped by divisive political policies.

We are at a time in American—and perhaps world—history when the strides in sports activism are particularly relevant as they speak to the spike in social protest and activism today, and also to the potential positive outcomes of those protests. Lately, we have seen the power of protest, and of organizing and unifying, not only to incite change but also to heal divisions. Athletes and the sports community have historically been a critical component in raising awareness, starting a dialogue, and healing our nation at pivotal moments. *Ways of Grace* has illustrated how numerous athletes are rallying for social change, and using their platform to draw awareness to issues that are important to them, or they feel are unfair or may alienate or marginalize large segments of the country.

With the election of Donald Trump as president, we have seen a surge in activism, inside and outside of the sports world. After the presidential inauguration, there was an uptick in social protest by star athletes. After their historic Super Bowl win, six New England Patriots—Martellus Bennett, LeGarrette Blount, Chris Long, Alan Branch, Dont'a Hightower, and Devin McCourty—decided to skip the celebratory White House visit because of new alienating political policies and rhetoric. These players' actions were called racist; however, Chris Long is white, and from the teammates' comments in the media, their decision was not about race; it was about inclusion and fighting against policies that divide instead of unite.

It is refreshing to me to see some of the greatest and most visible athletes take a stand with the platform they have been given. For instance, pro wrestler John Cena lent his voice to a #WeAreAmerica commercial about celebrating diversity. Steph Curry, typically laid-back, refused to be silent when Under Armour CEO Kevin Plank spoke out in support of Trump and called him "an asset." Uncharacteristically, Curry shot back, saying he agreed if you remove the "-et" at the end of "asset." According to the *Mercury News*, Plank told Curry the comments about Trump were meant "exclusively from a business perspective."

Curry was joined by pro wrestler and actor Dwayne "The Rock" Johnson, who signed a co-branding deal with Under Armour in 2015. Johnson posted on his Facebook page about

Plank [...] and lacking in perspective. . . . Inad[...] on where the personal political opi[...] partners and its employees were ov[...] nts of its CEO." Misty Copeland, t[...] rincipal dancer with the American [...] Under Armour spokesperson. She [...] page: "I have always appreciated the [...] rm that Under Armour has given me [...] unity, gender, and career on the world [...] ngly disagree with Kevin Plank's recent comments [...] t of Trump as recently reported. Those of you who have supported and followed my career know that the one topic I've never backed away from speaking openly about is the importance of diversity and inclusion. It is imperative to me that my partners and sponsors share this belief."

Today, inarguably, we are living in a more and more divided country. At the start of 2017 there were peaceful protests almost every day. The International Women's March the day after the presidential inauguration was the biggest worldwide protest ever in terms of participation. America is speaking up because so many of us feel empowered yet powerless at the same time. Hillary Clinton's winning the popular vote but losing to Trump's Electoral College win made millions of Americans feel as though their voices do not count the way they expect they should. But the rise of social media and subsequent protests and their positive effects gave a boost to citizens who want to believe that in this country, the people will always have the power over corporations and special interests. Case in point: Bowing to social pressure from the #DeleteUber campaign, Uber CEO Travis Kalanick withdrew from the president's Strategic and Policy Forum economic panel. Kalanick also pledged to donate three million dollars and immigration lawyers to help Uber drivers. That is people making a difference with action.

The country is becoming more engaged and active, and Americans can take a page out of the history of sports activism, and from sports activists—past and present—to inform their actions. With Trump as president, athletes are finding their voice when it comes to activism, in the same way citizens around the country are finding their voice—rallying, uniting, and inciting change.

This surge in activist athletes speaks to the fact that we have a point of view and are not afraid to speak out about issues we are passionate about. It is also a wake-up call for many fans to realize that the athletes they idolize have interests off the field of play. We are informed, socially conscious, and socially aware, and we strive to make a difference. We are a part of the world we live in. We are immigrants, minorities, male, female, ethnically diverse, and we have families and concerns like everyone else. Often athletes are thought to have only one skill, and it is usually sports-related. But we are intelligent, savvy, and deeply conscious of the world we live in and of our community. And if we are not informed about an issue that speaks to us, we seek guidance and advice. This is what Colin Kaepernick did when he spoke to Dr. Harry Edwards before going public with his protest. Yes, we are fallible, because we are learning this whole protest thing along the way. But our concerns speak to the country, to our community, and to its people, and we want to make a difference and give back for all that we have been given.

The misconception that athletes, in general, are not well rounded, articulate, or informed was repeated often while I was on tour. The simplest things caught fans by surprise, as though they didn't expect me to know anything outside of tennis. At times, it seemed fans thought athletes only exist for the few hours a day that we are on TV or playing our sport. Now, as a sports commentator, I'm seeing what is an intriguing combination of fans wanting to know more about athletes off the field, and athletes wanting to be more educated and well rounded. Fans realize and appreciate the talent, drive, hard work, and tremendous dedication athletes need to rise to the top of their game. When they reach that pinnacle, it is inspiring for me to see that so many want to use it as a springboard to help others who do not have the same opportunities, resources, or networks.

Diversity and Equality

When professional athletes take a stand, their organizations, franchises, and sponsors often follow. A January 2017 article by *Business Insider*, titled "Nike's CEO Condemned Trump's Immigration Order in a Letter to Staff," states: "Nike chief executive Mark Parker has condemned Trump's executive order banning arrivals from certain Muslim countries in an internal email to staff in which he said he was 'moved' by Sir Mo Farah's 'powerful statement.'"[1]

British long-distance runner Farah is a four-time Olympic gold medalist and a Nike brand ambassador. Born in Somalia, Farah moved to Britain when he was eight years old. While training in Ethiopia he voiced concerns that he might not be allowed back into the US because of President Trump's proposed travel ban. Farah called the travel ban "ignorant and prejudiced" in a statement Farah posted on Facebook. "It's deeply troubling that I will have to tell my children that Daddy might not be able to come home—to explain why the President has introduced a policy that comes from a place of ignorance and prejudice."

Business Insider writes,

Parker's message called on staff to stand up for the brand's values of celebrating diversity which he said were being threatened by the president's decision to halt the entire US refugee programme and impose a 90-day travel ban for nationals from Iran, Iraq, Libya, Somalia, Sudan, Syria and Yemen.

"Nike believes in a world where everyone celebrates the power of diversity," said Parker. "Regardless of whether or how you worship, where you come from or who you love, everyone's individual experience is what makes us stronger as a whole."

Parker addressed Farah's concerns in the letter saying he was "thinking of everyone who is impacted, like Sir Mo Farah."

The [letter] said: "What Mo will always have—what the entire Nike family can always count on—is the support of this company. We will do everything in our power to ensure the safety of every member of our family: our colleagues, our athletes and their loved ones."

Parker's message concluded: "Now, more than ever, let's stand up for our values and remain open and inclusive as a brand and as a company."

Mark Parker joins an ever-growing list of CEOs who have spoken out against Trump's travel ban. Netflix CEO Reed Hastings called the executive order "unAmerican"[2] and said it would "make America less safe (through hatred and loss of allies) rather than more safe." Slack CEO Stewart Butterfield called Trump's actions "gratuitously evil."[3] eBay CEO Devin Wenig said the executive order "fundamentally contradicts our company's values and America's values." In an open letter, Starbucks CEO Howard Schultz announced that in response to the ban, Starbucks would hire 10,000 refugees. Airbnb also announced it would provide free housing to "refugees and anyone not allowed in the United States." Google and Apple have also voiced concerns about the ban. In response, Google created a $4 million humanitarian fund to aid organizations assisting immigrants affected by the ban.

Parker is not one to shy away from speaking his mind about diversity and inclusiveness. The July 2016 *Fortune* article "Read Nike CEO's Heartbreaking Letter to Employees About Race and Violence" reported that Parker wrote a letter to his 32,000 employees at Nike about "the troubling issues of race, violence and policing that remain top of mind in the U.S." Parker is also *Fortune*'s Businessperson of the Year.

The letter is excerpted below:

Like many of you, I'm struggling to make sense of the incomprehensible. We have experienced heartbreaking, disturbing and challenging times in the United States. I have watched with sorrow the events that took place across the U.S. The loss and pain experienced in Min-

nesota, Louisiana and Dallas have left communities, institutions and even the nation tested. Our thoughts are
with all those impacted and their families and friends.

Nike has a long history of supporting the marginalized
and those whose voice is not always heard. In many cases
our athletes have eloquently argued for change and to stop
the situation. Last night, at the ESPYs, we heard athletes
like LeBron James, Carmelo Anthony and Chris Paul pow-
erfully speak out about the issues facing society. Others,
like Serena Williams, have also made their voices heard.

As a company, I'm proud that Nike takes a stand on
issues that impact all of us, our athletes and society as
a whole. And I am proud that Nike stands against discrimination in any form. We stand against bigotry. We
stand for racial justice. We firmly believe the world can
improve. We are a diverse company and . . . are firmly
committed to making it more diverse and inclusive.

We cannot solve all these profound, longstanding and
systemic issues. However, one thing will always be clear:
discrimination in any form and racial injustice are de-
structive forces.

"There is every reason to believe that there are plenty of
Nike employees feeling pain and despair," *Fortune* writes. "The
company is extraordinarily diverse."

In a broad staffing and sustainability report released in
May, the company revealed that for the first time ever,
"minority" employees, a healthy mix of black, African
American, Hispanic, Asian, Pacific Islanders, and other

ethnic groups, are now 52% of their workforce. (Specifically, black/African American employees are 21% of Nike's staff in the U.S.; while Hispanic/Latino workers are 18%.)

Parker is adding his voice to those of his most famous athlete-partners, like Serena Williams, LeBron James, and Carmelo Anthony, who have all been effective advocates for equality, and have been willing to participate in frank discussions about race.

But it's more than just inspiration at a difficult time. That Parker is tackling this as a CEO, not just through the marketing lens of a powerful cultural force, appears to be an extraordinarily important development for the growing diversity and inclusion movement in corporate life.[4]

Nike is backing up its words with marketing dollars in a powerful "Equality" ad campaign featuring a multicultural, international group of Nike's top brand ambassadors. The campaign will utilize their powerhouse draw to further a message of equality, diversity, and acceptance during a time of divisiveness and exclusion.

Diversity Is an Asset

In the aftermath of the first thirty days of the Trump presidency, talent agency powerhouse William Morris Endeavor-International Management Group (WME-IMG) has publicly vowed to protect its company diversity. In the February 8, 2017, article "WME-IMG to Form Political Action Committee, Vows to Protect Company 'Diversity,'" the *Hollywood Reporter* writes,

"WME-IMG co-CEOs Ari Emanuel and Patrick Whitesell are Planning to Form a Political Action Committee." Emanuel, whose brother Rahm Emanuel is the mayor of Chicago, met with President Trump in November after his win and was said to have discussed cabinet appointments.

According to the *Hollywood Reporter*,

> No details about what issues the PAC would tackle were revealed in the email, which noted that the company would pledge to protect its "diversity" in the next several years.
>
> While the context of the memo is unclear, it arrives as companies have been emboldened in opposition to President Trump's executive order targeting travel from seven Muslim-majority countries to the United States.

After the meeting Emanuel emailed a company-wide memo to staff:

> No matter what side of the aisle you sit on or where you live in the world, the call for meaningful and sustained civic engagement is louder than ever.
>
> In the coming weeks, you will hear more from us about:
>
> - The formation of a federal political action committee (PAC) in the U.S.
> - Convening internal and external forums with politicians and allied stakeholders
> - Connecting our clients with elected officials

- Introducing company-wide matching policies to support donations of time and money
- Developing actionable public policy solutions

This company's greatest asset is the diversity of our backgrounds and beliefs. Please know that we will do everything in our power to support and protect this diversity now and in the months and years ahead.[5]

WME-IMG represented Trump and also bought Miss Universe from him. This is an interesting nexus between business and social policy.

The Way Forward

The title "Ways of Grace" is a tribute to one of my all-time favorite books, *Days of Grace*, by Arthur Ashe. I thought often of his words while researching these trailblazing athletes and their inspiring, illuminating, and uplifting stories. I like to think that Ashe would have been as proud of this book as I am proud of everything he accomplished. His passion for helping others far outweighed his talent on the tennis court. That is saying a lot, considering he was a Wimbledon and US Open champion.

His book, *Days of Grace*, made me think long and hard about what I wanted to do with my life. I read it before having any success on the ATP Tour, but I knew if I did ever have anywhere near Ashe's success, that I wanted to use it as a way to make a difference. I hope *Ways of Grace* will have a similar positive effect on others—professional athletes, successful entrepreneurs, CEOs—who have reached a position of power, prestige, affluence, or influence, and who know that the end goal is to reach back, and to reach out, to make life better for others, for society, and for the world. Know that I continue to be lifted by your strides and achievements, and also by the efforts and accomplishments of anyone who has ever spoken out, organized, rallied, marched, or fought against what they saw as injustice, inequality, or inequity.

As Arthur Ashe said, "From what we get, we can make a living; what we give, however, makes a life."

Acknowledgments

I would like to thank Carol Taylor. Without her, this book would most likely be a jumbled mess of my never-ending thoughts and lack of structure. She put up with my busy schedule and even my kids taking me away from some of our talks. Thank you for helping me put my thoughts on paper. I am extremely pleased with how we worked together, and if this turns out well I know a lot of it is because of you.

I need to thank Matt Harper and Tracy Sherrod of Harper-Collins and Lisa Queen of WME-IMG. They had the idea for this book before I even realized that I wanted to write it. I am so glad they encouraged me to put down my thoughts in this form.

The athletes who took the time to speak with me on the record about activism were enlightening. I know how valuable time is to these busy athletes, so I want to thank Martina Navratilova, Billie Jean King, Meb Keflezighi, Chris Kluwe, and Aisam-Ul-Haq Qureshi for being such willing participants in this still-evolving experience.

Carlos Fleming has been integral in this process and my entire career. His official title is my agent, but that doesn't begin to describe his importance and value to me. I respect him for how well he has done his job as my agent, but I love him so much more as a friend. That will always be the most important part of our relationship. I cannot stress how much more that means to me than any deal he has ever done for me. I know they all took a lot of hard work on his part, but to me, what was more important is that he put that hard work in because he cared about me as more than a client. Thank you for that work and all the sacrifices, Carlos.

My parents shaped me to be the person I am today. So I have to thank them for making this seem like a formality to talk about activism and how people in athletics can make the world a better place. My mother and father stressed education first, and then tennis, which was the number one hobby in our house. There was plenty of talk about all sports, and a constant theme in our household was giving back. Because of the way I grew up, this all seemed exceedingly normal to me. I did not know there would be any other option once I had success on tour except to help others with the resources I gained from each match I won. So I want to thank them for instilling that mind-set in me from a very young age.

Last, but certainly not least, and certainly most important is my wife. There are only so many hours in the day, and I wish I could spend them all with my amazing family. I appreciate the patience my wife has with me. The research for this book took me away from my family at times, and I felt nothing but support from her. She is the best mom our two daughters could ever dream of having, and that makes it easier for me to take time away for a project like this that I find to be important. I could never think about taking any time away from them if this wasn't the case, so without her, this book never would have even been an option for me. Thank you, Emily.

Notes

Introduction

1. Benjamin Mueller and Nate Schweber, "Officer Who Arrested James Blake Has History of Force Complaints," September 11, 2015, www.nytimes.com/2015/09/12/nyregion/video-captures-new-york-officer-manhandling-tennis-star-during-arrest.html.
2. Nate Scott, "Broncos Linebacker Brandon Marshall Takes Knee During National Anthem," September 8, 2016, http://ftw.usatoday.com/2016/09/broncos-brandon-marshall-takes-knee-national-anthem-colin-kaepernick.
3. Marc Tracy, "Inside College Basketball's Most Political Locker Room," November 16, 2016, https://www.nytimes.com/2016/11/17/sports/ncaabasketball/wisconsin-badgers-nigel-hayes.html?smprod=nytcore-iphone&smid=nytcore-iphone-share&_r=0.
4. Julie Bosman and Mitch Smith, "Chicago Police Routinely Trampled on Civil Rights, Justice Dept. Says," January 13, 2017, https://www.nytimes.com/2017/01/13/us/chicago-police-justice-department-report.html.

Chapter 1: Early Trailblazers

1. Bill Christine, "Jockey Julie Krone More Than Holds Own on Track," February 03, 1988, http://articles.latimes.com/1988-02-03/sports/sp-27085_1_julie-krone.

2. "Mexico 1968," Olympic.org, https://www.olympic.org/mex ico-1968

3. Dave Zirin, "Australian Government Will Issue Overdue Apology to 1968 Olympic Hero Peter Norman," *The Nation*, https://www.thenation.com/article/australian-government -will-issue-overdue-apology-1968-olympic-hero-peter-norman.

4. Australian Olympic Committee, "Peter Norman not shunned by AOC," November 6, 2016, http://corporate.olympics.com .au/news/peter-norman-not-shunned-by-aoc.

Chapter 2: Changing the Game

1. Mbiyimoh Ghogomu, "The Quickest Possible Explanation of the Current Israeli-Palestinian Conflict," July 10, 2014, http:// thehigherlearning.com/2014/07/10/quickest-possible-expla nation-of-the-current-israeli-palestinian-conflict.

2. "This Day in History: May 14, 1948: State of Israel Pro- claimed," History.com, http://www.history.com/this-day-in -history/state-of-israel-proclaimed.

3. Peter Foster, "Muslim Who Plays with Jew Faces Tennis Ban," *The Telegraph*, July 2002, www.telegraph.co.uk/news/uknews /1398984/Muslim-who-plays-with-Jew-faces-tennis-ban .html. See also Mbiyimoh Ghogomu, "The Quickest Possible Explanation of the Current Israeli-Palestinian Conflict," *The Higher Learning*, July 2014, http://thehigherlearning.com/2014 /07/10/quickest-possible-explanation-of-the-current-israeli -palestinian-conflict.

4. Foster, "Muslim Who Plays with Jew Faces Tennis Ban."

5. "Syrian President Bashar al-Assad: Facing Down Rebellion," BBC News, October 21, 2015, www.bbc.com/news/10338256.

6. Ibid.

7. "Who We Are," website of the Fédération Internationale de Football Association (FIFA), www.fifa.com/about-fifa/who -we-are/index.html.

8. Ibid.

9. Juliet Macur, "Long Before Kaepernick, There Was Navratilova," *New York Times*, October 16, 2016, www.nytimes.com /2016/10/17/sports/martina-navratilova-colin-kaepernick-pro test.html.

10. Lauren Collins, "The Third Man," *The New Yorker*, September 2013, www.newyorker.com/magazine/2013/09/02/the-third -man-8.

11. Ksenija Pavlovic, "World Tennis No.1 Novak Djokovic Talks to Spectator Life ahead of Wimbledon," *The Spectator* (UK), June 22, 2013, www.spectator.co.uk/2013/06/home-game.

Chapter 3: You Run Like a Girl

1. A. Uhlir, "The Wolf Is Our Shepherd: Shall We Not Fear?" *Phi Delta Kappan* 64, no. 3 (November 1982): 172–76.

2. E. J. Vargyas, *Breaking Down Barriers: A Legal Guide to Title IX* (Washington, DC: National Women's Law Center, 1994).

3. M. J. Festle, *Playing Nice: Politics and Apologies in Women's Sports* (New York: Columbia University Press, 1996).

4. M. McKeown, "Women in Intercollegiate Athletics," in *The Need For a National Study of Intercollegiate Athletics: A Report to the American Council on Education*, G. H. Hanford, ed., vol. 2, pp. 369–87 (ERIC Document Reproduction Service no. ED 132 968).

5. Festle, *Playing Nice*; Uhlir, "The Wolf Is Our Shepherd."

6. K. L. Hill, "Women in Sport: Backlash or Megatrend?" *Journal of Physical Education, Recreation, and Dance* 64, no. 9 (November/December 1993): 49–52.

7. Vargyas, *Breaking Down Barriers*, 6.

8. Robert B. Everhart and Cynthia Lee A. Pemberton, *The Institutionalization of a Gender Biased Sport Value System*, Winter 2001, www.advancingwomen.com/awl/winter2001/everhart _pemberton.html.

Chapter 4: Shut Up and Play

1. Chris Kluwe, "I Was an NFL Player Until I Was Fired by Two Cowards and a Bigot," *Deadspin*, January 1, 2014, https://deadspin.com/i-was-an-nfl-player-until-i-was-fired-by-two-cowards-an-1493208214.
2. Ibid.
3. Tom Pelissero, "Former Vikings Punter Chris Kluwe Plans to Sue Team," *USA Today*, July 15, 2014, www.usatoday.com/story/sports/nfl/vikings/2014/07/15/chris-kluwe-lawsuit-discrimination-mike-priefer/12674611.
4. Ibid.
5. Ben Goessling, "Chris Kluwe, Vikings Avoid Lawsuit," ESPN.com, August 19, 2014, www.espn.com/nfl/story/_/id/11375100/chris-kluwe-minnesota-vikings-reach-settlement-avert-lawsuit.
6. Josh Levin, "Colin Kaepernick's Protest Is Working," *Slate*, September 12, 2016, www.slate.com/articles/sports/sports_nut/2016/09/colin_kaepernick_s_protest_is_working.html.
7. Nate Boyer, "An Open Letter to Colin Kaepernick from a Green Beret-Turned-Long Snapper," *Army Times*, August 30, 2016, www.armytimes.com/articles/nate-boyer-colin-kaepernick-commentary-flag-national-anthem-protest-nfl.

Chapter 5: More Than Just a Game

1. Julie Bosman and Mitch Smith, "Chicago Police Routinely Trampled on Civil Rights, Justice Dept. Says," January 13, 2017, www.nytimes.com/2017/01/13/us/chicago-police-justice-department-report.html.
2. Jesse Washington, "Still No Anthem, Still No Regrets for Mahmoud Abdul-Rauf," *The Undefeated*, September 1, 2016, https://theundefeated.com/features/abdul-rauf-doesnt-regret-sitting-out-national-anthem.
3. Ibid.

Epilogue

1. Tony Connelly, *The Drum*, "Nike's CEO Condemned Trump's Immigration Order in a Letter to Staff," January 30, 2017, www.businessinsider.com/nikes-ceo-condemned-trumps-immigration-order-in-a-letter-to-staff-2017–1.

2. Todd Spangler, *Variety*, "Tech CEOs Blast Trump Muslim Immigration, Travel Ban: 'So Un-American It Pains Us All,'" January 28, 2017, http://variety.com/2017/digital/news/netflix-apple-google-trump-muslim-immigration-ban-1201972448/.

3. Judd Legum, *Think Progress*, "Starbucks' Epic Response to Trump's Executive Order," January 29, 2017, https://thinkprogress.org/starbucks-epic-response-to-trumps-executive-order-a9d2cd8f9786.

4. Ellen McGirt, "Read Nike CEO's Heartbreaking Letter to Employees About Race and Violence," July 15, 2016, Fortune.com, http://fortune.com/2016/07/15/nike-ceo-letter-race-police.

5. "WME-IMG to Form Political Action Committee, Vows to Protect Company 'Diversity'," by Erik Hayden, Hollywood Reporter.com, February 2017, www.hollywoodreporter.com/news/wme-i-img-form-political-action-committee-vows-protect-company-diversity-973353.

Bibliography

Introduction

Ashe, Arthur, and Arnold Rampersand. *Days of Grace: A Memoir.* New York: Ballantine Books, 1993.

Chapter 1: Early Trailblazers

Welday Walker's letter to the Tri-State league was published in *Sporting Life*, March 14, 1888.

Bartyzel, Monika. "Girls on Film: 11 Female Athletes Who Deserve Their Own Sports Biopic." *The Week*, April 12, 2013. https://theweek.com/articles/465658/girls-film-11-female-athletes-who-deserve-sports-biopic.

ACTIVISM STORIES: BIG AND SMALL MOMENTS

Smith, Tommie, Delois Smith, and David Steele. *Silent Gesture: The Autobiography of Tommie Smith.* Philadelphia: Temple University Press, 2007.

Dunlap, Tiare. "Iconic 1968 Olympic Activist Tommie Smith Defends Colin Kaepernick's National Anthem Protest: 'He's Bringing the Truth Out.'" *People*, August 31, 2016. http://people.com/sports/olympic-activist-tommie-smith-defends-colin-kaepernick.

Salute. Written, directed, and produced by Matt Norman, 2008.

GAME. SET. MATCH.

"Billie Jean King Tennis Champion & Activist." Makers.com. www.makers.com/billie-jean-king.

"About The WTA." Women's Tennis Association. www.wtatennis .com/scontent/article/2951989/title/about-the-wta.

King, Billie Jean. *Pressure Is a Privilege: Lessons I've Learned from Life and the Battle of the Sexes*. New York: LifeTime Media, 2008.

———. "This Tennis Icon Paved the Way for Women in Sports." TED Talk. May 2015. www.ted.com/talks/billie_jean_king _this_tennis_icon_paved_the_way_for_women_in_sports.

Wilson, Theo. "Billie Jean King Admits the Affair." *New York Daily News*, May 2, 1981. www.nydailynews.com/sports/more-sports /billie-jean-king-confesses-1981-lesbian-article-1.2615020.

Chapter 2: Changing the Game

HOW SPORTS CHANGES PERCEPTIONS AND LIVES

A Beautiful Game. Directed and produced by Sarah Cordial. Fox Sports special.

CREATING CHANGE, QUIETLY

Martina Was Alone on Top. ESPN Special.

Lipsyte, Robert, and Peter Levine. *Idols of the Game: A Sporting History of the American Century*. Atlanta: Turner Publishing, 1995.

SERBIA: THE SWIMMING POOL ALUMNI

Folley, Malcolm. "War-Torn Past of the Serbian Smasher Ana Iva-novic." *Daily Mail*, July 1, 2007. www.dailymail.co.uk/femail /article-465391/War-torn-past-Serbian-smasher-Ana-Ivanovic .html.

van Heerden, Lashara. "A Girl's Dream Becomes a Woman's Suc-cess: Ana Ivanovic on Overcoming Adversity and Empower-

ing Others." Quercus Foundation News, March 8, 2016. www
.quercusfoundation.org/news/a-girls-dream-becomes-a-womans
-success-ana-ivanovic-on-overcoming-adversity-inspiring-others.

Chapter 3: You Run Like a Girl

Everhart, Robert B., and Cynthia Lee A. Pemberton. *The Insti-tutionalization of a Gender Biased Sport Value System*. Winter 2001. www.advancingwomen.com/awl/winter2001/everhart _pemberton.html.

PUBLIC PERCEPTION OF FEMALE ATHLETES

Rodrick, Stephen. "Serena Williams: The Great One." *Rolling Stone*, June 18, 2013. www.rollingstone.com/culture/news/se rena-williams-the-great-one-20130618.

Boren, Cindy. "Serena Williams: 'If I Were a Man,' I Would Have Been Considered the Greatest a Long Time Ago." *Washington Post*, December 26, 2016. www.washingtonpost.com/news /early-lead/wp/2016/12/26/serena-williams-if-i-were-a-man-i -would-have-been-considered-the-greatest-a-long-time-ago.

"Serena Williams Sits Down with Common to Talk about Race and Identity." *The Undefeated*, December 19, 2016. http://theunde feated.com/features/serena-williams-sits-down-with-common -to-talk-about-race-and-identity.

Williams, Serena. "'We Must Continue to Dream Big': An Open Letter from Serena Williams." *Guardian*, November 29, 2016. www.theguardian.com/lifeandstyle/2016/nov/29/dream-big -open-letter-serena-williams-porter-magazine-incredible-women -of-2016-issue-women-athletes.

Sreedhar, Anjana. "The inspiring Story of How Venus Williams Helped Win Equal Pay for Women Players at Wimbledon." *Women in the World*, July 10, 2015. http://nytlive.nytimes.com /womenintheworld/2015/07/10/the-inspiring-story-of-how -venus-williams-helped-win-equal-pay-for-women-players-at -wimbledon.

Chapter 4: Shut Up and Play

Ayanbadejo, Brendon. "Same Sex Marriages: What's the Big Deal?" *Huffington Post*, May 25, 2009. www.huffingtonpost.com/bren don-ayanbadejo/same-sex-marriages-whats_b_190591.html.

Kluwe, Chris. "An Open Letter to Emmett Burns." *Huffington Post*, September 7, 2012. www.huffingtonpost.com/chris-kluwe/an -open-letter-to-emmett-burns_b_1866216.html.

Linskey, Annie. "Burns Backs Off Bid to Silence Ravens Player." *Baltimore Sun*, September 9, 2012. www.baltimoresun.com/news /maryland/politics/bs-md-burns-backlash-20120909-story .html.

Collins, Jason. "Why NBA Center Jason Collins Is Coming Out Now." *Sports Illustrated*, May 6, 2013. www.si.com/more-sports /2013/04/29/jason-collins-gay-nba-player.

Williams, Charean. "Michael Sam: 'I'm Not the Only Gay Person in the NFL.'" *Fort Worth Star-Telegram*, March 26, 2015. www .star-telegram.com/sports/nfl/dallas-cowboys/article16442273 .html.

It Gets Better Project, ItGetsBetter.org.

Chapter 5: More Than Just a Game

Bosman, Julie, and Mitch Smith. "Chicago Police Routinely Trampled on Civil Rights, Justice Dept. Says." *New York Times*, January 13, 2017. www.nytimes.com/2017/01/13/us/chicago -police-justice-department-report.html.

Lichtblau, Eric, and Jess Bidgood. "Baltimore Agrees to Broad Change for Troubled Police Dept." *New York Times*, January 12, 2017. www.nytimes.com/2017/01/12/us/baltimore-police -consent-decree.html.

Oppel, Richard A. Jr., Sheryl Gay Stolberg, and Matt Apuzzo. "Justice Department to Release Blistering Report of Racial Bias by Baltimore Police" *New York Times*, August 9, 2016. www

.nytimes.com/2016/08/10/us/justice-department-to-release
-blistering-report-of-racial-bias-by-baltimore-police.html.

Guardian police killings database. "People Killed by the Police in
the US." www.theguardian.com/us-news/ng-interactive/2015
/jun/01/the-counted-police-killings-us-database.

Washington Post police killings database. "Fatal Force." www
.washingtonpost.com/graphics/national/police-shootings-2017.

McGrath, Timothy. "American Police Kill Civilians at a Shocking Rate Compared to Other Developed Countries." *Los Angeles Daily News*, May 4, 2015. www.dailynews.com/government
-and-politics/20150504/american-police-kill-civilians-at-a
-shocking-rate-compared-to-other-developed-countries.

Alexander, Michelle. *The New Jim Crow: Mass Incarceration in the
Age of Colorblindness*. New York: The New Press, 2012.

Chapter 6: A Personal Choice

"I'm Not a Role Model." *Newsweek*, June 27, 1993. www.news
week.com/im-not-role-model-193808.

Index

About the Author

JAMES BLAKE has been a professional tennis player since 1999, when he left Harvard to play full time. He retired from the sport in 2013. In 2015, he became chairman of the USTA Foundation. He grew up in Fairfield, Connecticut, and lives in San Diego, California, with his wife and daughters.

CAROL TAYLOR is a bestselling author who has written nine books. A former Random House book editor, she lives in New York.

ALSO BY
JAMES BLAKE

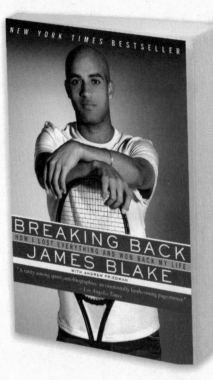

BREAKING BACK
HOW I LOST EVERYTHING AND WON BACK MY LIFE
Available in Paperback and eBook

"The grace and dignity that James has shown during some very difficult times has been a source of great inspiration." —Andre Agassi

In *Breaking Back*, Blake provides a remarkable account of how he came back from terrible heartbreak and self-doubt to become one of the top tennis players in the world. A story of strength, passion, courage, and the unbreakable bonds between a father and son, *Breaking Back* is a celebration of one extraordinary athlete's indomitable spirit and his inspiring ability to find hope in the bleakest of times.